Collins
English for Business

SMALL TALK
Deborah Capras

Collins

HarperCollins Publishers
77–85 Fulham Palace Road
Hammersmith
London W6 8JB

First edition 2014

10 9 8 7 6 5 4 3 2 1

© HarperCollins Publishers 2014

ISBN 978-0-00-754623-7

Collins® is a registered trademark of HarperCollins Publishers Limited

www.collinselt.com

A catalogue record for this book is available from the British Library

Typeset in India by Aptara

Printed in China by South China Printing Co. Ltd

MIX
Paper from
responsible sources
FSC
www.fsc.org **FSC™ C007454**

FSC™ is a non-profit international organisation established to promote the responsible management of the world's forests. Products carrying the FSC label are independently certified to assure consumers that they come from forests that are managed to meet the social, economic and ecological needs of present and future generations, and other controlled sources.

Find out more about HarperCollins and the environment at
www.harpercollins.co.uk/green

Contents

Contents map

4

	Tips / Remember this	Language focus	Next steps
- I'm sorry, but I didn't catch your name. - I'm sorry, but what was your last name again? - How do you spell your name? - Am I saying it correctly? - Let me give you my business card.	- All about names - Handshakes - Business card etiquette	Avoiding 'How do you do?'	Make flashcards for learning vocabulary
- I can't believe we haven't met before. - I'm sorry, but can you jog my memory? - I'm really sorry, but what was your name again? - Actually, I don't think we've met. - Oh, I'm so sorry! I thought you were someone else.	Reconnecting with people	- 'Remember' or 'remind'? - Idiomatic language	Try different learning styles
- The keynote speaker certainly gave me some food for thought. - Hi. Is this seat taken? - Do you mind if I join you? - I know what you mean. - No, it's free. Please join us. - Not at all. Please do.	Body language	- Tag questions - Vocabulary for conferences	Prepare well before going to a conference or event
- I'm looking for new suppliers. - I'm here to talk to clients. - That must be interesting. - What about you?	Building a conversation step by step	Talking about work and your profession	Learn to talk about your job in English
- You know, I think we might have something you'd be interested in. - Would you be interested in meeting up after the conference? - Look, here's my card. Why don't you give me a call? - That would be great. - Yes, I'd like that.	Body language	Questions	Use the SMART method to improve your English
- Can I take your coat? - Can I offer you something to drink? - The flight was fine. - Your directions were great. - Thank you. That's very kind of you. - How far is it to the office?	- Attitudes to time and dress code - Travel small talk	International travel	Learn about tourist sites in your area
- What languages do you speak at home? - Didn't your daughter move to Shanghai? - How did you end up in Russia? - It's kind of you to ask. - Congratulations! - I'm so sorry to hear that.	- Avoiding stereotypes - Being sensitive		Learn 'word families'
- Any plans for tonight? - How often do you go to concerts? - Really? That's a coincidence! I also ... - No way! So do I. - I've never tried it, but I'd like to.	Finding common ground	Paying and responding to compliments	Learn vocabulary related to hobbies and interests

5

	Chapter title	Aims	Key phrases
9	Who's who and what's what	- Introduce a visitor to colleagues - Give a company tour - Show interest in how my business partner works	- I'd like to introduce you to the team. - Come and meet Tom. He's our Sales Manager. - Let me explain how our organization works. - Let me give you a tour of our department. - Accounts are on the top floor.
10	Entertaining	- Entertain and be entertained - Make and accept invitations - Feel confident about making small talk in a restaurant	- Would you like to join me for dinner this evening? - That would be great. - Is there anything I need to know before I make a reservation? - Do you need any help with the menu? - Can you recommend something else?
11	Tell us a story	- Tell interesting stories - Use humour in small talk - Show interest in stories	- I'll never forget the time I ... - Funny you should say that, but a similar thing happened to me. - It was before we had mobiles. - You're not going to believe this, but ... - You should have seen their faces!
12	Sensitive topics	- Make small talk without causing offence - Discuss sensitive topics - Deal with insensitive questions	- This is a little embarrassing, but we don't normally do that. - To be honest, I'd prefer not to talk about it. - To tell you the truth, I wouldn't know. - You know, I really couldn't say. - Don't worry about it.
13	Goodbye – for now!	- End a conversation politely - Make people want more - Look to the future	- Anyway, I'd better be going if I want to catch my flight. - It was a pleasure to meet you. - Give me a call the next time you're in London. - It's been really nice talking to you again.
	Part B: At a distance		
14	Phone, video and online meetings	- Make small talk on the phone or via video conference - Contribute in group virtual meetings - Explain and deal with technical problems	- Hi, it's Joe. - How are you this morning, Pete? - Are you busy? Is this a good time to talk? - How are things at the head office? - What's the time difference again? - We're three hours behind. - It's been great talking to you.
15	Email exchanges	- Begin and end an email with small talk - Maintain good relationships through email - Switch to business after small talk	- Morning John - I hope you're well. - Thank you for your kind hospitality. - Hope you had a good break. - I've just got back from Finland and it was fabulous.
16	Social media for professionals	- Invite someone to connect - Post messages and comments - Share articles and updates	- You may not remember me, but we spoke briefly at the BON conference in Dubai last month. - Thanks very much for the invite. - I use Facebook just with close friends and family. Let's connect on LinkedIn® instead.

	Tips / Remember this	Language focus	Next steps
- Most people work from home one day a week. - You're lucky to have a canteen in the building. - Thank you for showing me around.	- Structuring small talk - Corporate culture - Giving and receiving gifts	Recommending colleagues	Learn vocabulary to talk about your company
- You should try the vegetables. - It was fabulous, but I couldn't possibly eat any more. - Thanks for bringing me here. It's been a wonderful experience. - My pleasure. I'm so glad you like the food.	Entertaining in different cultures	- Paying the bill - Refusing food politely	Revise regularly
- Anyway, in the end, ... - You're joking, right? - How terrible! - I'm not surprised. - Were you all right?	- Structuring your story - Jokes and humour	Past tenses	Learn how to tell a good story
- No need to apologize. - I totally understand. - Sorry. I had no idea. - I apologize. You must think I'm terribly insensitive. - I'm so sorry to hear that.	- Dealing with difficult topics - Taboo gestures	Contradicting politely	Learn how to read a news story about a place you are visiting or interested in
- Please excuse me. I have to make a phone call. - Right, then. We'll be in touch soon. - Thanks again for your hospitality. - See you soon.	- Checking contact details - Body language: closing a conversation	- Closing a conversation - Future forms	Improve your English during 'dead' time
- I'll let you get back to your work. - Actually, you've caught me at a bad time. - We're all here. This is Philippe. I'm here with John and Julie. - John's running a little late. - Let's get started. - That's it for today.	Video conferences and online meetings	Describing technical problems	Use your mobile phone and the internet to improve your English
- Have a good weekend. - See you on Monday. - Very best wishes - All the best - Kind regards	Writing professional emails	Changing the subject	Learn new words and phrases from emails you receive
- I thought this article might interest you. - I thought of you when I read this. - Great article. Thanks for sharing. - Congratulations on your new job! - Well done! I'm sure you'll be a success.	- Networking and raising your profile - Using Facebook and Twitter		Use social media to improve your English

About the author

Deborah Capras is an experienced and respected Business English author, editor, trainer and teacher trainer. She has been working in the industry for over 20 years. In addition to her experience in Business English training, she has also worked as the marketing manager for a European-Japanese company. She has written for *Business Spotlight*, Germany's leading magazine for learners of Business English, since its launch in 2001 and has been the deputy editor of the magazine since 2009.

Introduction

Small talk is not small

We all prefer to do business with people we trust. To build trust with your business partners, you need to have good working relationships and you can create the basis for such relationships if you can connect with people on a personal level. Small talk can help you to make this connection.

Why make small talk?

- **To create a bond:** By opening up about your interests, you can create a more personal bond with someone and therefore a better relationship.
- **To create a network:** You can find the best business partners in business situations and at social events. If you can engage with strangers using small talk, you can create a network of people you can call on for their expertise. And they, in turn, will want to add you to their networks.
- **To create a positive atmosphere:** You can use small talk to make yourself and others feel at ease.

What factors influence small talk?

Place

The way you make small talk with a stranger at a conference is different from the way you talk to someone who is visiting your office or someone at an evening event. If you are welcoming a visitor to your office, you need to make them feel at ease. At a conference, you are on neutral ground and can use small talk simply to make contacts. At an evening event, you are also on neutral ground and the situation is more likely to be relaxed. Therefore, topics may be more personal.

Personality

According to the Myers-Briggs Type Indicator®, a popular tool that identifies people as belonging to distinctive personality types, some people are more extroverted and others are more introverted. Extroverts enjoy social events and group conversations with lots of different people. They become energized in social situations, often moving quickly from one topic of conversation to another. Introverts, on the other hand, prefer one-on-one conversations. They will often talk about fewer topics, but in more detail. They may be better at keeping in touch at a distance, via email for example. They aren't necessarily bad at small talk, but they may find it harder and more tiring; they may be better listeners. So does this mean that introverts and extroverts can't talk to each other? Not at all. If you are an extrovert, give the introverts time to join in. If you are introverted, make the most of your one-on-one interactions. By the way, no one type is seen as good or bad – they are just different.

Relationship

To some extent, the kind of small talk you make depends on the status of the person you are talking to. It is generally more relaxed between people who have a similar status than, for example, between a receptionist and a CEO. Small talk could still be important, but it may be more limited.

The longer you know someone, the friendlier and more informal small talk can be. Less formal language helps to build personal relationships. If you are too formal, you may create a distance that is hard to bridge.

Gender

For many years Deborah Tannen, a sociolinguist and author of *You Just Don't Understand: Women and Men in Conversation*, has been studying how men and women communicate and interact. She describes the type of talk that men make as 'report-talk'. By this, she means that they like to exchange information about impersonal topics. Women, however, generally prefer 'rapport-talk', which focuses on personal relationships and is more intimate. She also notes that men tend to talk more in public than women.

Culture

What are your cultural values? Do you know what values are important to your business partner? The closer your values, the more you will have in common and the easier it is to make small talk. Culture is influenced by many different factors, including language, religion, societal norms and traditions. Knowing your business partner's cultural values may help you to decide which topics you can discuss together.

Fons Trompenaars, a leading expert on intercultural communication and author of *Riding the Waves of Culture: Understanding Cultural Diversity in Business*, has studied the extent to which our cultural values affect the way we interact with people and how we do business. He uses the terms 'specific' and 'diffuse' to describe how people from different cultures view their professional and private lives.

In 'specific' cultures such as the Netherlands and Switzerland, people like to keep their private lives private. They believe that relationships are important, but not necessary to do business. In 'diffuse' cultures such as China, India, Russia and Spain, private and professional lives are closely linked. People from these cultures believe that a good personal relationship is vital to doing business and they often spend time socializing outside of work.

Be prepared to make small talk

We make small talk based on what is happening around us, what is important to us, our experiences and our feelings. Small talk is often spontaneous and random, so it is difficult to predict what people will talk about. You need to have a passive understanding of many expressions to follow many small talk exchanges, but you can take part using a much smaller set of key phrases.

This book will go a long way towards helping you to learn key phrases for a variety of situations. It also presents the language that you are likely to hear, especially when talking to native speakers of English.

How to use this book

The language level of this book is B1–B2 on the Common European Framework of Reference, equivalent to intermediate–upper-intermediate level.

This book can be used as a self-study guide or as part of a course. Work through each chapter in order or refer to a specific chapter before you go to a conference, to a meeting or to the office of a business partner and focus on the key phrases you will need. Use the book as a resource when you know you will have the opportunity to meet people and to make small talk in English.

Overview

Part A: Face to face

As most small talk interactions are face to face, most chapters focus on this type of communication.

Part B: At a distance

There are long periods of time between face-to-face meetings when you need to communicate and build on your relationship via email or on the phone. Nowadays, with a lot of business conducted via email, you may have business partners that you never meet face to face. Nevertheless, it is still important to make use of small talk opportunities.

Part C: Communication strategies

This part has tips and suggestions on how to improve your general communication strategies. There is also a special focus on body language and how to spell out names and email addresses.

Answer key

There is a comprehensive answer key at the back of the book.

Audio

All audio for this book is available free online. Go to www.collinselt.com/businessresources to listen to it.

On the website you will notice that we have two different types of audio. First, all key phrases and scenarios have been recorded in a studio as a model for you to follow. You can listen to this audio and repeat the phrases to practise your pronunciation and intonation. We have also recorded real-life audio. By this we mean real people using small talk on location (i.e. not in the studio). In this audio, you will hear people using 'um' and 'uh' when they are thinking about what they want to say. You will also hear different accents. Listening to this real-life audio is good practice as it increases your awareness and sensitivity to different speakers of English. There are full transcripts of the real-life audio online so you can read along while you are listening.

Chapter structure

My goals
There are three clear goals for each chapter.

Quiz
Before you can start to improve your small talk skills, you need to think about what you can do and where you need help. Answer the questions in the self-awareness quiz honestly.

Study focus
Each chapter focuses on one area of small talk. This section sets the scene and tells you what to look out for.

Key phrases
The key phrases are a vital section of each chapter. These are common phrases that you should learn because they will give you the confidence to deal with many kinds of small talk situations. The key phrases are highlighted so that they are easy to find. For example, before you go to a networking event, you could look up the key phrases you would need to make small talk there.

To start with, you may only want to learn to use one key phrase for each situation and simply recognize the others when you hear them. As you gain confidence, you can learn to use more key phrases. You can listen to all the key phrases in Part A online.

Scenarios
This section has dialogues and written communications that show you how the key phrases are used in context. You can listen to all the Part A dialogues online.

Over to you
You need to practise to make progress. This section has exercises that give you the chance to practise the new language and personalize what you learn.

Language focus
Many of the chapters have a section that explains a specific language point. These sections focus on the kind of language you might hear and will need to understand, and they also look at aspects of grammar.

Remember this!

Here you will find additional information about the topic of the chapter, such as details about culture, traditions and common business practices.

Tips

Here you will find useful tips on what you can do to improve your small talk skills.

Next steps

This section has useful advice on how to improve your study skills.

Finally ...

Make sure you try out the language you have learnt in real business situations and don't worry too much about making mistakes. Generally, people don't pay a lot of attention to language errors, but they won't forget someone who is showing an interest in them and is interesting to talk to. That is what small talk is really all about.

1

New contacts

My goals
- Make a good first impression
- Greet people I've never met before
- Check names and help people to remember mine

Quiz

Ask yourself: 'What kind of first impression do I make?'

	Absolutely	Sometimes	No, I don't
I find it easy to introduce myself to someone I've never met before.	☐	☐	☐
I look people in the eye and smile when I greet them.	☐	☐	☐
When I meet people for the first time, I tell them my first and last name.	☐	☐	☐
I speak clearly and with confidence.	☐	☐	☐
I find it easy to remember people's names.	☐	☐	☐

Study focus

At conferences, networking events and even in the office – wherever you do business – you will meet new people. How do you make a good first impression? A warm, friendly greeting will help you. Using small talk to start a conversation will help too. Try to make sure that people remember you and try to remember them too. You might not hear their name properly the first time, and in this chapter you will learn how to ask people to repeat their name.

Key phrases

Making the first move
I don't think we've been introduced. My name's Hans, Hans Schiller.
Hi, I'm Mary, Mary Smith.
We haven't actually met, but I'm Hans Schiller.
May I introduce myself? I'm Mary Smith.
I don't think we've met. I'm Mary Smith.

Giving the right response
It's a pleasure to meet you.
Pleased to meet you.
(It's) good/great/nice to meet you.
(It's) good/great/nice to meet you too.

Checking names
I'm sorry, but I didn't catch your name.
I'm sorry, but what was your last name again?
How do you spell your name?
'Athanasis'. Am I saying it correctly?

Helping people to remember your name
Please, call me John.
Let me give you my (business) card.
Here's my (business) card.

 Go to www.collinselt.com/businessresources
to listen to the key phrases.

Scenarios

Rena:	Hi, **I don't think we've met. I'm Rena Chioti.**
Antonio:	**Nice to meet you, Ms Chioti. Am I saying it correctly?**
Rena:	Yes, but **please, call me Rena.**
Antonio:	Rena. **I'm Antonio, Antonio Messina.**
Rena:	**Good to meet you too, Antonio. How do you spell your name?** Is it with double 's'?
Antonio:	Yes, like the city in Sicily. My family's from there.

Rob:	**We haven't actually met, but I'm Rob Williams.**
Markus:	**It's a pleasure to meet you. I'm Professor Kern, Markus Kern.**
Rob:	**It's good to meet you too.**
Markus:	**I'm sorry, but I didn't catch your last name.**
Rob:	It's Williams, as in Robbie Williams. You know, the singer. **Let me give you my business card.**
Markus:	Thank you. And here's mine.

Jules:	Hello. **I don't think we've been introduced. My name's Jules, Jules Chirac.**
Sergei:	Oh, I'm sorry, Jules! Sandra, this is Jules Chirac, our designer in our French office. Jules, this is Sandra Harper. She's with RTV.
Sandra:	**Nice to meet you, Jules.** I've seen your work. It's impressive.
Jules:	Thank you. That's great to hear. **It's nice to meet you too.**

 Go to www.collinselt.com/businessresources
to listen to the scenarios.

Over to you

1 Match the sentence beginnings with the sentence endings.

1	I'm sorry, but I	**a**	been introduced.
2	Let me give you	**b**	meet you.
3	I don't think we've	**c**	didn't catch your name.
4	May I	**d**	introduce myself?
5	It's a pleasure to	**e**	my business card.

2 John is talking to Sayuri when Ria joins them. Put the dialogue in the correct order.

....**1**.... **Ria:** Hello. I don't think we've been introduced. My name's Ria.

.... **Sayuri:** Actually, I'm a fan of your blog, Ria.

.... **John:** Oh, I'm so sorry, Ria! Sayuri, this is Ria Fisher, our company blogger in London. We work in the same building.

.... **John:** Ria, this is Sayuri Riisa. She's one of our engineers here in Berlin.

.... **Ria:** It's great to meet you too, Sayuri.

.... **Sayuri:** Nice to meet you, Ria.

....**7**.... **Ria:** Really? Thank you. It's nice of you to say that.

3 Check your understanding. Answer the questions about the dialogue in exercise 2.

1 Where are they? ....

2 Who works in the UK? ....

3 Who is a writer? ....

4 Who works in Germany? ....

5 Has Ria met John before? ....

6 Does Sayuri know Ria? ....

....

4 Complete the sentences with the correct form of the verbs in the box.

| catch | give | introduce | meet | say | spell |

1 I don't think we ....
2 'Sahinda'. Am I .... it correctly?
3 May I .... myself?
4 Let me .... you my card.
5 I'm sorry, but I .... your last name.
6 Could you .... your last name for me?

5 Complete the dialogue.

You: **(1)** *(Say that you don't know each other and give your name.)*

....

....

Paul: It's a pleasure to meet you. I'm Paul Mathews.

You: **(2)** *(Respond to the greeting and say that you didn't hear Paul's last name.)*

....

....

Paul: It's Mathews. But please, call me Paul. I'm sorry, but how do you spell your name?

You: **(3)** *(Spell your name and offer your business card. If possible, say something about your name to help Paul to remember it.)*

....

....

6 Can you say the letters of your name in English?

Language focus: How do you do?

Avoid using the old-fashioned phrase **How do you do?** It can sound solemn and too formal. If someone *does* use it to greet you, the fixed response is **How do you do?**

Remember this! Handshakes

- The purpose of a handshake is to show respect and to perform a greeting ritual.

- Not everyone shakes hands, but in international business situations and contexts, a handshake when greeting someone is common.

- People from different cultures may expect different greetings, especially in their own countries. In Japan you may be greeted with a bow. In some countries, in particular in the Middle East and India, it is best not to offer your hand in greeting, especially to women.

- In some countries people may shake hands more often than in others. In Germany, for example, people often shake hands when they meet for the first time, when they leave and then every time they meet again, even if it is the next day. In the UK, however, people may only shake hands when they meet for the first time. Observe how people behave and do the same.

- Asian people usually have a gentle handshake. Americans generally expect handshakes to be firmer.

- If you are unsure what to do, wait for the other person to initiate the handshake.

- Don't hold on to a person's hand for too long. It can make them feel uncomfortable.

- Don't use both your hands to shake someone's hand. This may make the other person feel that you think you are more important than them.

- Don't shake hands so roughly or firmly that you could hurt someone – and don't shake hands very weakly either. What people will remember positively is a short, fairly strong handshake.

Tips: All about names

- For a warm and friendly greeting, tell people your first name as well as your last.

- If someone says their last name first, they probably expect you to use it (e.g. 'Mr Smith').

- If someone gives you their title, they expect you to use that too (e.g. 'Dr Chen').

- Someone with a more senior position in an organization might prefer to use last names.

- Repeat the person's name as soon as you can.

- If you didn't catch someone's name, ask for it again.

- Say something about your name to help people to remember it.

Remember this! Business card etiquette

- Exchanging business cards should be part of the conversation. Generally, people don't hand out cards until they have been introduced.

- Take enough cards with you to meetings and events. It is unprofessional to say you don't have any (more) with you.

- Keep your cards in a case – they stay cleaner. And know where they are. People who can't find their cards look disorganized.

- Give and receive cards with your right hand. In Asia people often like to give and receive cards using both hands. By showing respect to the cards, you show respect to each other.

- Make sure that your card is the right way round and the right way up when you hand it to the person you are talking to.

- You can add a note to your own card, but it is best not to write on someone else's, especially in Japan. People there may find this impolite. If you need to write something on it to help you to remember the person, do so later.

- Try to make a positive comment about some aspect of a person's card, such as the company logo or the colour.

Next steps

You don't need a large vocabulary to make a good impression during your first introduction. Make sure you can use the key phrases in this chapter so that you have the confidence to talk to people at business and social events.

To help you to prepare, write the phrases that you would like to use on separate cards. On the back of the cards, write key words from the phrases.

For example:

CALL ME	Please call me (your name).
CATCH	I didn't catch your last name.
CARD	Here's my card.
INTRODUCE	May I introduce myself?
MET	I don't think we've met.
PLEASURE	It's a pleasure to meet you.
SAYING	Am I saying your name correctly?
SPELL	How do you spell your name?

 Go to www.collinselt.com/businessresources to listen to the real-life audio for this chapter.

2

Old contacts

My goals
- Greet people I've met in the past
- Greet people I haven't seen for a long time
- Politely admit that I don't remember someone

Quiz

Ask yourself: 'Are you well prepared for the next time you meet?'

	Absolutely	Sometimes	No, I don't
I know what to say when I see someone again after a long time.	☐	☐	☐
If I think I know someone, I have the confidence to introduce myself to them.	☐	☐	☐
I know what to say to someone I've been emailing but never met face to face.	☐	☐	☐
I always say I remember someone, even when I don't.	☐	☐	☐
If someone gets my name wrong, I find it hard to correct them.	☐	☐	☐

Study focus

In business your first face-to-face contact with someone might come after you have already communicated with that person by email, by phone or even through social media networks. If you have worked in the same industry for a while, you will often meet the same people again and again – sometimes after long periods. The way you greet these people will be different from the way you greet a stranger. It is a good idea to remind them of your relationship.

Key phrases

Meeting someone you know unexpectedly
It's Katsumi, isn't it? I'm Sue Jones. We met last May.
You're Katsumi, right? Sue.

Meeting someone you know after a long time
Long time no see! / How are you/things? / How have you been?

Responding
That's right.
I'm great/good. How about you?
Good to see you again.

Meeting someone you 'know' but have never met
You must be Paul. I recognize you from your website.
You must be Paul. I recognized your voice immediately!
It's so great/good/nice to finally meet you.
(It's) great/good/nice to meet you at last.
I can't believe we haven't met before.

Admitting you don't remember someone
I'm sorry, but can you jog/refresh my memory?
I'm really sorry, but what was your name again?
I'm sorry. Where was it we met?

Correcting someone if they get your name wrong
Actually, it's Mark.
Actually, I don't think we've met.

Apologizing
I'm sorry. I remember now. How could I forget!
Oh, I'm so sorry! I thought you were someone else.

 Go to www.collinselt.com/businessresources
to listen to the key phrases.

Scenarios

Mary:	**It's Katsumi, isn't it? Mary. We met last May.**
Katsumi:	**I'm sorry, but can you jog my memory?**
Mary:	Mary Smith. We met at the conference in Brighton. I used your mobile phone when my battery ran out.
Katsumi:	Oh, Mary! Of course. **I'm sorry. How could I forget!** You used it to call friends in Australia.
Mary:	I called a taxi!
Katsumi:	Just kidding. **It's good to see you again.** How are you?
Mary:	**I'm good,** really good. **How about you?**

Paula:	Hi. You must be Ghada.
Ghada:	**That's right.**
Paula:	**I recognize you from your photo on the website.** I'm Paula, from Marketing.
Ghada:	Paula! Of course. **It's so good to finally meet you. How are things?**
Paula:	Great. **I can't believe we haven't met before.**
Ghada:	Me neither.

Beate:	**You're Martin, right? Beate.** From Switzerland.
Mark:	**Actually, it's Mark. I don't think we've met.**
Beate:	**Oh, I'm sorry! I thought you were someone else.**
Mark:	No problem. Anyway, it's nice to meet you. I'm Mark Jones.
Beate:	Beate Schmidt.

 Go to www.collinselt.com/businessresources
to listen to the scenarios.

Over to you

1 Put the words in the correct order to make useful expressions. Don't forget to add punctuation.

1 time / see / no / long

....

2 see / good / you / again / to

....

3 have / you / how / been

....

4 to / so / you / meet / good / it's / finally

....

2 Complete the questions with the words in the box.

about	been	right	things

1 You're Katsumi, ... ?

2 How are .... ?

3 How have you .... ?

4 How .... you?

3 There is one word missing in each of the expressions below. Rewrite the expressions with the missing word in the correct position.

1 I'm sorry. How I forget!

....

2 I thought you were someone.

....

3 I can't we haven't met before!

....

4 I'm sorry, but can you my memory?

....

4 **The following exchange did not go well! Rewrite it to make it more polite.**

Paula: It's Jonathan, right?

John: No, not Jonathan. John.

Paula: I'm Paula Reed. We met at the conference in Hong Kong.

John: I don't remember you.

Paula: We sat next to each other at the dinner.

John: It's possible.

Paula: It's good to see you again.

John: Is it?

Try again, John.

Paula: It's Jonathan, right?

John: ....

Paula: I'm Paula Reed. We met at the conference in Hong Kong.

John: ....

Paula: We sat next to each other at the dinner.

John: ....

Paula: It's good to see you again.

John: ....

5 **Complete the dialogues with key phrases.**

1 **A:** You're Rio, right?

 B: ....

 A: Oh, I'm sorry. I thought you were someone else.

 B: ....

2 **A:** Hi. You must be (your name).

 B: ....

 A: I recognized you from the website.

 B: ....

 A: I'm Ioannis Papandreou. From Finance.

 B: ....

Language focus: 'Remember' or 'remind'?

The verbs **remember** and **remind** may come in useful when you meet someone you know. Do you know the difference?

Remember

- If you **remember people, events or things**, you know them. You have an idea of them in your mind and are able to think about them.
  *I'm really sorry, but I can't **remember** your name.*

- **Remember** is followed by the **-ing** form of the verb when you talk about things you did in the past.
  *Oh yes, I **remember** talking to you in Prague.*

Remind

- If you **remind someone** about something, you make that person remember it.
  *Could you **remind** me again where we met?*

- If you say that **someone reminds you of** another person or thing, you are saying that they are similar to them.
  *You **remind** me of a colleague of mine.*

Idiomatic language

For non-native speakers, idiomatic language can be difficult to understand. Listen out for idiomatic greetings and notice how people generally respond. At first, you may not feel confident enough to use such expressions, but you should expect to hear them and be able to react to them.

Idiomatic greetings	Responses
Fancy meeting you here!	*What a lovely/pleasant surprise!*
What have you been up to?	*Not a lot. I'm hanging in there.*
How are you keeping?	*I'm good, really good.*
My goodness, it's been a while!	*Hasn't it (just)!*
Sorry, but your name escapes me.	*It's Brian Glazer.*

Scenario

Brian: Fancy meeting you here, Louise!

Louise: Brian! What a pleasant surprise! Long time no see! Gosh, how long has it been?

Brian: Too long! At least a year. What have you been up to?

Louise: Not a lot, really. What about you?

Brian: Oh, hanging in there, you know.

Tips: Reconnecting with people

If you have already been in contact with people, you need to reconnect with them when you meet face to face. Here are some tips.

Do's

- Say your name – in case they don't remember it.

- Shake the person's hand. If you know the person reasonably well, double-cheek kisses are common between women. However, men should wait for a woman to signal that kisses are OK.

- Make the first move if you think you know someone. If you are right, you will make someone feel good. If not, you will make a new contact. You have nothing to lose!

Don't's

- Don't worry if you have forgotten someone's name. Instead, try to recall a few details about your last meeting; this will make your forgetting the name less impolite. And do ask them to remind you of their name. If you avoid using their name altogether, it might be obvious that you have forgotten it.

- Don't forget to say how you know the person. If it is a surprise meeting, they may need a polite reminder.

- Don't feel bad if someone doesn't remember meeting you before. It happens.

Next steps

Have you ever thought about how you like to learn? Do you like to work with visuals such as pictures or videos? Do you learn better when you listen to new language? Or do you need to do something active to learn? It is a good idea to try out a variety of learning styles and find what works for you. Here are a few suggestions.

- When you write down the language you would like to learn, use pens of different colours to highlight difficult words or expressions.

- Draw pictures to help you to remember vocabulary. Or imagine a situation where you could use the vocabulary and visualize the scene. Where are you? What are people wearing? How are they standing?

- Listen to the audio recordings of key phrases and scenarios online. As you listen, pause the recording and repeat the phrases.

- Record yourself on your smartphone. Listen to yourself and think about how you speak. Are you too fast or too quiet? Do you sound enthusiastic or bored? Be honest!

- Write vocabulary and key phrases on cards and keep them on your desk. Use two cards for each key phrase. Write half a phrase on one card and the rest of the phrase on another card. Then play 'Memory' during your coffee break. Put all the cards face down on a desk. Turn over one card and then turn over a second card. Do they make a key phrase? If they do, keep them. If they don't, turn them both over, shuffle the cards and start again.

- Learn vocabulary while you are travelling. Buy different coloured envelopes for your vocabulary cards. Put the cards with the vocabulary you don't know in a red envelope, the vocabulary you aren't sure of in a yellow one and the vocabulary you know well in a green one. Move the cards to different envelopes as you learn the vocabulary.

- Write key phrases on pieces of paper and stick them on the fridge in your kitchen.

 Go to www.collinselt.com/businessresources to listen to the real-life audio for this chapter.

3

Start networking

My goals
- Strike up conversations at conferences
- Respond to strangers who greet me
- Become more confident at making the first move

Quiz

Ask yourself: 'How do I make use of networking opportunities?'

	Absolutely	Sometimes	No, I don't
I return from conferences with lots of new contacts.	☐	☐	☐
I know lots of different ways to start a conversation.	☐	☐	☐
I'm friendly and open to people who talk to me.	☐	☐	☐
As soon as a presentation finishes, I leave.	☐	☐	☐
I find it easy to join a group of people I don't know.	☐	☐	☐

Study focus

Conferences, trade fairs and events are the perfect places to network. The people you meet there may be able to help you and your business in the future – and you may be able to help them too. But it can only happen if you strike up conversations with strangers. This can be scary at first, but this chapter provides you with the language you need to do this, together with helpful tips and advice.

Key phrases

In the exhibition hall

Is this the first time you've been to this conference/trade fair?

Are you giving a talk later? I think I recognize you from the programme.

Are you waiting to go into the workshop/presentation?

The venue/atmosphere is amazing/great/outstanding, isn't it?

The weather here has been fantastic/terrible, hasn't it?

After a presentation or workshop

(That was a) good/great/nice session. I got a lot out of it.

That was thought-provoking/entertaining/impressive.

The keynote speaker certainly gave me some food for thought.

He/She made some valid points, don't you think?

He/She knows his/her stuff. I was impressed.

It's been a long day.

In the break

Hi. Is this seat taken?

(Do you) mind if I join you?

Hi there. Is there room for one more at this table?

Responses

Absolutely. / Exactly.

I know what you mean. / I agree. / That's so true.

I know exactly how you feel. / I know the feeling.

No, it's free. Please join us. / Not at all. Please do.

Of course/Sure. Take/Have a seat.

Giving your name

I'm Dana Dardari, by the way.

By the way, my name's Peter. Peter Graham.

 Go to www.collinselt.com/businessresources
to listen to the key phrases.

Scenarios

Nasir: Well, **the keynote speaker certainly gave me some food for thought.**

Breda: **She was impressive** – and **she knows her numbers.**

Nasir: Definitely. I loved her accent. She's Irish, isn't she?

Breda: Yes, she is. And so am I.

Nasir: I thought so. **Are you giving a talk later? I think I recognize you from the programme.**

Breda: Yes, I am. My session is at two.

Nasir: Oh! I'm going to it. **I'm Nasir Mazhar, by the way.**

Breda: Breda Houlihan. It's nice to meet you, Nasir.

Lesia: **Mind if I join you?** The other tables are full.

Charlotte: **Of course.** I'll just move my bag for you.

Lesia: Thanks. I've been on my feet all day!

Charlotte: **I know the feeling.** I left home at four this morning.

Lesia: That *is* early. So you're not from Edinburgh.

Charlotte: No, no. I'm from Avignon.

Lesia: That's such a beautiful place! **I'm Lesia, by the way.**

Frank: **Hi there. Is there room for one more at this table?**

Holger: **Of course. Please join us.**

Frank: I really need a coffee. I'm running out of energy.

Holger: **I know what you mean. It's been a long day.** Just one more session.

Frank: I feel sorry for the presenters who have the last one.

Holger: Well, the organizers put the best speakers in the last session, so actually, I feel sorry for *us*.

Frank: **That's so true. By the way, I'm Frank.**

 Go to www.collinselt.com/businessresources to listen to the scenarios.

Over to you

1 Match the questions with the correct polite responses.

1	Is this seat taken?	**a**	Of course.
2	Mind if I join you?	**b**	Yes, it is.
3	Is there room for one more at this table?	**c**	Not at all.
4	Is this the first time you've been to this trade fair?	**d**	No, it's free.

2 Longer responses sound better. What can you add to make the responses in exercise 1 friendlier?

1 Of course. ....

2 Yes, it is. ....

3 No, it's free. ....

4 Not at all. ....

3 What can you say to start a conversation? Match the sentence beginnings with the sentences endings.

1	Are you giving	**a**	from the programme.
2	I think I recognize you	**b**	to go to the workshop?
3	Is this your first	**c**	a talk today?
4	Are you waiting	**d**	time at this venue?

4 Complete the words in the sentences.

1 This **v** _ _ _ **e** is great.

2 The **at** _ _ _ _ _ _ _ **e** is amazing, isn't it?

3 The **k** _ _ _ _ _ **e** speaker was good, wasn't she?

4 She certainly gave me some food for **th** _ _ _ _ **t**.

5 Choose the correct word.

1 Her presentation was **impressive / impressed**.

2 She made some **valid / correct** points.

3 His talk was really **interested / interesting**.

4 The weather here has been **impressed / terrible**, don't you think?

5 It's been a(n) **outstanding / valid** event.

6 What can you say to show that you agree with someone? Put the words in the correct order. Don't forget to add punctuation.

1 I / what / know / mean / you

....

2 feeling / the / know / I

....

3 feel / how / know / you / I / exactly

....

4 true / so / that's

....

7 Complete the dialogue.

Frank: Hi there. Is there room for one more at this table?

You: **(1)** *(Respond in a positive and friendly way.)*

....

Frank: I really need a coffee.

You: **(2)** *(Respond and then make a comment about the last presentation.)*

....

....

Frank: Absolutely! It certainly gave me food for thought.

You: **(3)** *(Agree in a friendly way and then make a comment about the venue.)*

....

Frank: Yes! It's much, much better than last year.

Language focus: Tag questions

Tag questions are very useful when you want to strike up a conversation. We use them if we expect someone to agree with what we are saying. They make the listener feel like they have something in common with the speaker. They are easy to respond to and can lead to longer conversations.

We make tag questions by adding question tags to statements. If the statement has a positive verb, we use a negative question tag. Here are some common tag questions that can be used to strike up a conversation.

> The food here is great, **isn't it?**
> (It's a) great venue, **isn't it?**
> (It was an) interesting programme, **wasn't it?**
> (This is an) amazing place, **isn't it?**
> Horrible/Lovely weather, **isn't it?**
> (It's) busy, **isn't it?**

In small talk try to respond in a positive way whenever possible. It is best to answer with more than just 'Yes, it is'. Try to make a further comment so that the conversation can flow more easily.

> A: Horrible weather, isn't it?
> B: Yes, it's much worse than I expected.
>
> A: Interesting programme, isn't it?
> B: Very. There are so many talks I'd like to go to.
>
> A: Long line, isn't it?
> B: Yes. The coffee must be good!

If the statement has a negative verb, we use a positive question tag.

> A: It isn't very busy, **is it?**
> B: No, it isn't. I expected more people to be here.

Remember this! Body language

How can you be successful at starting a conversation with someone you don't know? Pay attention to people's body language before you start talking to them. Are they smiling? Are they looking around the room? Are they making eye contact with you? If the answer is 'yes', they may be easy to talk to. On the other hand, if they are looking down at their feet or standing alone, apart from other people, they may be more difficult to talk to. Remember, people may be asking the same questions about you. If you have the right body language, people will come up and talk to you too.

Language focus: Conferences

Here are some basic terms to talk about conferences and trade fairs.

- **attend (a presentation):** *This is the first time I've attended a workshop on social media.*

- **cloakroom/restroom:** *Do you know where the cloakroom is? I'd like to leave my bag there.*

- **delegate:** *This is my first time here as a delegate.*

- **elevator/lift:** *I hope there's a lift. The next talk is on the fourth floor.*

- **exhibit hall:** *I'm looking for the exhibit hall. Is it down this way?*

- **exhibitor:** *We might register as exhibitors next year.*

- **keynote speaker:** *The keynote speaker was impressive, wasn't she?*

- **main auditorium:** *Is this the way to the main auditorium?*

- **panellist:** *The panellists are clearly experts on computer viruses.*

- **presenter:** *I thought the presenter made some useful points.*

- **session:** *The last session is usually the most interesting one.*

- **site plan:** *Can I have a quick look at your site plan? I'm looking for the information desk.*

- **venue:** *This is a fantastic venue.*

Next steps

Be prepared for a conference or event. You will need to make preparations anyway, but try to think about how you can use these preparations to improve your small talk at the event. Before you go:

- find out what the weather will be like so that you can think about the kind of tag questions you could use to start a conversation.

- look up the names of the speakers. Conference programmes often have photographs of the speakers too. You might see these people during the break and have a chance to use the key phrase 'I think I recognize you from the programme'.

- go online and check out the venue. Is there anything special about the building? Did a famous architect design it, for example? Was it used for something else before it was turned into a conference venue? Does it have an interesting history? Is there something interesting about it that you could discuss?

- You may not have time to travel around the city where the conference is taking place, but you might have time to talk about the city with people who know it well. Find out about one or two important places or events before you go so that you can discuss them if you have the chance.

- Make sure you can describe how you travelled to the event. People often like to compare their journeys or their experiences, especially if the conference is somewhere that is difficult to reach.

If you feel prepared, you will feel – and look – more confident when you strike up a conversation.

 Go to www.collinselt.com/businessresources to listen to the real-life audio for this chapter.

4 Introducing the business

My goals

- Describe my work briefly and in an interesting way
- Show an interest in others
- Find something in common with others

Quiz

Ask yourself: 'Do I describe my work in the best possible way and show an interest in other people's work?'

	Absolutely	Sometimes	No, I don't
I know what to say after I've introduced myself.	☐	☐	☐
I know how to explain why I'm attending an event.	☐	☐	☐
I feel it's best to keep details about my career path to myself.	☐	☐	☐
I know how to describe what I do in a few sentences.	☐	☐	☐
I prefer to let my business partner ask the questions.	☐	☐	☐

Study focus

Once you have struck up a conversation with someone, you can move on to talk about work. When they first meet someone, people generally describe their work briefly so that everyone has a chance to talk and learn something about each other. The important thing is to listen for something that you have in common with the person you are talking to and, if possible, to make a comment about it.

Key phrases

Finding a business connection

I see from your name tag that you work for Miles Inc.
Do you work for ABC? / Are you based nearby?
So, what do you hope to get out of this conference?
So, what brings you to this talk?

Showing interest in someone's work

What line of business are you in?
What (exactly) do you do?
How long have you been working for ABC?

Talking about your career

Well, I'm in finance/marketing/banking/retail.
I've been there for four years now. / I've been working there since January.
I joined them a year ago. Before that I was with Barks.
I used to work in Russia/sales.
I'm self-employed. / I'm a freelancer.
I'm responsible for/I'm in charge of our website.
I run our online marketing.

Describing your goals for the event

I'm looking for new programmers/suppliers.
I'm here to talk to clients/licensees.
I'm looking into/I'm interested in the latest trends/copyright issues.

Showing interest and talking about a connection

Really? / That's interesting. / That must be interesting.
Maybe you know … / Maybe you've heard of …
What about you?

 Go to www.collinselt.com/businessresources
to listen to the key phrases.

Scenarios

Hans: I see you have a Miles Inc. bag. **Do you work for them?**

Nisha: **I used to**, and I still use the bag.

Hans: I'm Hans, by the way, Hans Müller. **I joined Miles Inc. about a year ago** as an engineer.

Nisha: **Really?** Nice to meet you, Hans. I'm Nisha Parekh. **So, what brings you to this conference?**

Sylvia: **I see from your name tag that you work for ABC.**

Raffi: Yes, I do. I work in the Madrid offices.

Sylvia: I work for ABC too, but I'm based here. **I'm in finance.**

Raffi: **Really? Maybe you know Robert Smith.**

Sylvia: Of course I do.

Raffi: **I used to work** with him. Is he here today?

Sylvia: Yes, he is. I'll call him and ask him to join us.

Raffi: That would be great.

Marco: **So, what do you do?**

Damien: I work in the energy sector. I'm a designer.

Marco: **Really? What exactly do you do?**

Damien: **I run the company's advertising campaigns.**

Marco: **That must be interesting. And what do you hope to get out of this conference?**

Damien: **I'm looking for new ideas for design software. What about you?**

Marco: **I'm a freelance programmer.**

 Go to www.collinselt.com/businessresources to listen to the scenarios.

Over to you

1 **Are the statements about the past or the present?**

		Past	Present
1	I used to work in sales.	☐	☐
2	I joined the company two years ago.	☐	☐
3	I've been with the company for a year now.	☐	☐
4	I'm in banking.	☐	☐
5	I've been working there since March.	☐	☐
6	Before I joined the company, I used to be a teacher.	☐	☐

2 **Complete the sentences with your own words.**

1 I used to work in ....

2 I joined .... ago.

3 I've been with .... for .... now.

4 Before I joined .... , I used to be a(n) ....

5 I've been working at .... since ....

3 **Complete the sentences with one word in each gap.**

1 I'm in charge .... Marketing.

2 I'm responsible .... online sales.

3 I'm interested .... learning more about copyright laws.

4 I'm looking .... the latest trends.

5 I'm here to talk .... our suppliers.

4 Put the words in the correct order to make questions. Don't forget to add punctuation.

1 of / you / what / out / hope / event / to / do / this / get

....

2 conference / this / so / what / to / brings / you

....

3 you / business / line / are / what / in / of

....

4 you / there / been / how / have / working / long

....

5 Complete the dialogue with the words in the box and make it sound friendlier.

exactly	really	so	that must be	well	what about

Francesco: **(1)** .... , what do you do when you're not going to conferences?

Kuniko: **(2)** .... , I work in the luxury goods business, but I'm a lawyer, not a designer.

Francesco: **(3)** .... ?
What **(4)** .... do you do?

Kuniko: I'm in charge of our licensees in Asia.

Francesco: **(5)** .... interesting. And what do you hope to get out of this conference?

Kuniko: I'm looking for new partners.
(6) .... you?

Francesco: I'm a designer.

6 Write short responses to the questions about you.

1 **A:** So, what line of business are you in?
  B: ....

2 **A:** What exactly do you do?
  B: ....

3 **A:** So, what brings you to this conference?
  B: ....

Language focus: Talking about work

Exactly

- **What/Where/When** etc. **exactly** is generally used to ask for more details about something. It can also signal that you are genuinely interested in learning more about someone.

  What exactly do you do?

  However, if you stress **exactly** too much when you ask the question, you may sound rude, as if you don't take someone's job seriously.

- You can also use **exactly** in these questions.

  *Where **exactly** are you based?*
  *Where **exactly** are you from?*

Used to

- We use **used to + infinitive** to talk about past situations and habits that are not true any more.

  *I **used to work** for ABC, but now I'm a freelancer.*
  *I **used to be** a teacher.*

- We use **used to + infinitive** in positive statements. In negative statements we use **didn't use to + infinitive.** In questions we use **did(n't) + subject + use to + infinitive.**

  *We **didn't use to go** to a lot of conferences, but now we go to at least four every year.*

  A: ***Did** you **use to work** with Robert?*
  B: *Yes I did. Do you know him?*

- Don't confuse **used to + infinitive** with **be used to + -ing form**. We use **be used to + -ing form** to talk about things that we are familiar with or have become accustomed to.

  *At first it was hard, but now **I'm used to living** in Rio.*

Language focus: Your profession

Make sure you understand the terms for common industries. You may hear them in sentences like: **I work in ...**

- **the aerospace business.** (spacecraft, rockets, etc.)
- **the aviation business.** (planes, helicopters, etc.)
- **Hospitality and Catering.** (hotels, restaurants, etc.)
- **construction.** (building houses, offices, etc.)
- **the energy sector.** (the part of the economy that deals with energy such as gas, electricity, etc.)
- **entertainment.** (movies, theatre, TV shows, etc.)
- **health care.** (hospitals, doctors, clinics, etc.)
- **logistics.** (transporting goods, etc.)
- **the media.** (newspapers, the internet, television, etc.)
- **pharmaceuticals.** (medicine and drugs)
- **public relations.** (promoting a person or business)
- **the public sector.** (the part of the economy that is controlled by the government)

Next steps

If you want to work internationally, you will have to talk about your job in English, so make sure you are prepared for that moment. Remember that *you* are the expert in the area in which you work. You know what you do and you know what is important about your job; you just need to find the right words to talk about these things in English.

- Start with your job title. Do you know the correct version of your title in English? If you don't, find out if your company has a policy on job titles and ask if there is one that you should use. If there isn't, look at the titles that people use in similar positions. Could you use any of them? Check with your company before you use a title in emails or when introducing yourself. You could also ask a native speaker friend or colleague for advice.

- Some titles don't tell people enough about your job, so make sure you can describe what you do in terms that people in your industry will understand – and also people who aren't in your industry.

- Check out the English websites of companies that you work for or with. Many have a list of job opportunities that may provide you with ideas for your job title and description.

- It is important that you understand the job titles and job descriptions of the people in your industry. On English-language job sites, search for jobs in companies in your industry. Filter your search according to department or specialist area until you find something that is similar to what you do. Is there a job title and description that you could use? Explain to your colleagues/manager what you are doing so that they don't think you are looking for a new job!

 Go to www.collinselt.com/businessresources to listen to the real-life audio for this chapter.

5 On to business

My goals
- Make a smooth transition to talking about business
- Ask questions with a business focus
- Explore business opportunities

Quiz

Ask yourself: 'How do I move from small talk to business?'

	Absolutely	Sometimes	No, I don't
I find it hard to change from basic small talk to small talk with a purpose.	☐	☐	☐
I know how to ask questions to get people talking about themselves and their business.	☐	☐	☐
I know how to move a conversation on to business naturally and smoothly.	☐	☐	☐
I make many contacts and I know how to follow up on them.	☐	☐	☐
I worry that my body language might be wrong.	☐	☐	☐

Study focus

What would happen if you were at a conference and you walked up to someone and immediately started asking them questions about their business? They might be surprised and they may even think that you are rude. This is why we start with small talk. But what happens when you have made small talk? How do you then move the conversation on to business in a way that doesn't sound forced or false? This is the focus of this chapter.

Key phrases

Moving from small talk to talking about business
So, do you travel much for work?
Are you working on anything interesting at the moment?
What's happening in your sector/industry right now?

Changing the topic
Actually, we're working on an interesting project right now.
By the way, my company is working on/developing/looking into …
Funny you should say that. I'm working on …
Speaking of copyright, do you know anyone who could advise us?
That reminds me, I think I heard that your company is …

Finding connections and business opportunities
Have you heard of them? / Maybe you've heard of us.
You have some great products.
May I ask if you know of any useful contacts?
Actually, we want to improve our system/change our focus.
You know, I think we might have something you'd be interested in.

Suggesting a follow-up
I can ask my colleague(s).
Maybe we could get together and discuss this in detail.
Would you be interested in meeting up after the conference?
Look, here's my card. Why don't you give me a call?
Well, I have your card, so I'll be in touch.

Responding
That would be great. / Yes, I'd like that.
(That) sounds like a good idea. / I'd be very interested in that.
That might work. / That could be interesting.

 Go to www.collinselt.com/businessresources
to listen to the key phrases.

Scenario

Geneviève: I'm based in Lyon, France, actually, but we also have offices in Madrid and Hamburg.

Hans: **Speaking of Germany**, do you do much business there?

Geneviève: We do. Germany is one of our biggest markets.

Hans: Ours too. **Are you working on anything interesting at the moment?**

Geneviève: We're developing a video game for BTT to use in their training. **Have you heard of them?**

Hans: I have. **Actually, we want to update our training programme** and were also thinking of using video games. What's the name of your company?

Geneviève: 333GameStudio.

Hans: Oh, I know it. **You have some great products** for pilots, I believe.

Geneviève: That's right. Who do you need to train?

Hans: Truck drivers.

Geneviève: **You know, I think we might have something you'd be interested in.**

Hans: **Maybe we could get together and discuss this in detail.**

Geneviève: **Look, here's my card. Why don't you give me a call?**

Hans: **Sounds like a good idea.** I'll call you next week.

 Go to www.collinselt.com/businessresources to listen to the scenario.

Over to you

1 **Read the dialogue and answer the questions.**

Pierre: So, do you travel much for work?

Igor: Quite a bit. I just got back from a week in Brazil.

Pierre: Really? What business are you in?

Igor: Pharmaceuticals.

Pierre: So am I. We're based in Ireland.

Igor: Oh, we work with an Irish company. They package our drugs for the Brazilian market.

Pierre: Funny you should say that. Our company also offers such a service. APPEUT is the name. Have you heard of us?

Igor: I haven't, actually.

Pierre: Would you be interested in meeting up after the conference? I could tell you more about our services.

Igor: That could be interesting.

1 What line of business are the speakers in?

....

2 What do the companies have in common?

....

....

3 Could they form a business relationship?

....

2 **What can you say to show interest? Complete the responses with the words in the box.**

be	like	sounds	work	would

1 That .... be great.

2 Yes, I'd .... that.

3 .... like a good idea.

4 I'd .... very interested in that.

5 That might ....

3 **What can you say to change the focus of a conversation? Complete the words in the sentences.**

1 A _ _ _ _ _ _ _ , we also need to update our system.

2 S _ _ _ _ _ _ _ **o** _ copyright, do you know anyone who could advise us in Peru?

3 Y _ _ **k** _ _ _ , I think we might have something you'd be interested in.

4 B _ **t** _ _ **w** _ _ , my company is working on a similar project.

5 T _ _ _ **r** _ _ _ _ _ _ **m** _ , I heard that your company is investing in such projects.

6 F _ _ _ _ **y** _ _ **s** _ _ _ _ _ **s** _ _ **t** _ _ _ . I'm working on a similar project at the moment.

4 **What can you say to suggest meeting up again? Put the words in the correct order. Don't forget to add punctuation.**

1 together / detail / could / get / and / we / this / maybe / discuss / in

....

2 here's / me / look / card / call / why / you / give / my / don't / a

....

3 have / well / in / I / so / touch / card / be / your / I'll

....

5 **Write short responses to the questions about you.**

1 A: Do you travel a lot for work?

B: ....

2 A: Are you working on anything interesting at the moment?

B: ....

....

3 A: What's happening in your industry right now?

B: ....

....

Language focus: Questions

It is important to ask the right questions so that you can find out what you have in common with others.

Closed questions

- Closed questions require a 'yes' or 'no' answer.
  Do you travel a lot for work?
  Are you working on anything interesting at the moment?

- You can answer closed questions with a simple 'yes' or 'no', but if you provide more information, you show your listener that you are interested in talking to them.

Open questions

- Open questions start with words like 'What', 'Where', 'When', 'Why', 'Who' and 'How' and require more detailed answers.
  What*'s your main focus?*
  Where *are your main markets?*
  Who*'s in charge of marketing at your company?*

- If you find that the person you are talking to works in the same industry as you, discuss trends in a general way at first. To begin with, try not to think too much about how you can make use of someone. An informal conversation can give you ideas for other business projects.

Polite questions

- To ask a polite question, you can use modal verbs.
  May *I ask if you would be interested in meeting after the conference?* (polite and formal)
  Would *you be interested in talking about this in more detail?* (polite and quite formal)
  Could *you recommend someone?* (more formal than 'Can you ...?')

Remember this! Body language

- **Mouth:** Smile.

- **Eyes:** Don't stare, but keep regular eye contact.

- **Head:** Nod your head (move it up and down) to show that you are listening. You can tilt your head slightly to the side to show that you are listening, but be careful. A tilted head and a big smile can look like you are flirting.

- **Hands:** Don't wave your hands around too much in a professional situation. Some people like to raise an index finger to signal that they would like to say something, but you can look aggressive if you start to point your finger at someone.

- **Arms:** Don't fold your arms in front of your chest. This creates a barrier and suggests that you aren't interested in getting to know the person you are talking to.

- **Legs:** When you are sitting down, try not to infringe on other people's personal space. This means that you should sit with your legs together and not stretched out. If you are a man and are sitting down, don't sit with your legs wide apart. When standing, you will be less intimidating if you stand slightly at an angle, to the side, and not face to face all the time.

- **Feet:** A tip for men in particular: don't cross your legs in such a way that the bottom, or soles, of your shoes are visible. This is considered extremely rude in Arab countries.

- **Body:** Relax and don't stand too close to people. There are different ideas about personal space, so it is best to be careful and to keep a distance of about an arm's length.

Next steps

Peter Drucker, an American management consultant, was probably the first person to use the term **SMART** as a business method. Project managers use it to focus on their objectives for a project. You can also use **SMART** to help you to improve your business English skills. As you would in a project, decide what you want to do and make sure that it is **SMART**.

S is for 'specific':

   What exactly do I want to improve?

M is for 'measurable':

   How can I measure my progress?

A is for 'achievable':

   Do I have the skills to do it, and will I make the effort?

R is for 'realistic':

   Am I expecting to do too much or not enough?

T is for 'time':

   How much time can I spend on it?

Here are some suggestions for **SMART** learning goals.

Specific: Focus on only one chapter of this book over a period of two weeks. Every day during this period focus on the key phrases or listen to the online audio.

Measurable: At the end of the two weeks, measure your progress. Do the exercises in the 'Over to you' section.

Achievable: You should spend 20–30 minutes studying every day. You could read, listen and learn vocabulary or test yourself on the key phrases.

Realistic: Each chapter has enough material for two weeks.

Time: If you don't have time to study every day, give yourself more time. You will only know how much time you really need once you start studying.

 Go to www.collinselt.com/businessresources to listen to the real-life audio for this chapter.

Great guests, perfect hosts

My goals

- Be a good guest and show interest in my host
- Be a great host and make my guests feel welcome
- Offer help and know how to respond

Quiz

Ask yourself: 'Do I make guests feel welcome and hosts feel appreciated?'

	Absolutely	Sometimes	No, I don't
I know what to say to make international visitors feel welcome.	☐	☐	☐
I feel nervous about greeting guests on their arrival.	☐	☐	☐
As a host, I offer help to business visitors with enthusiasm.	☐	☐	☐
When I'm a guest, I know how to respond to my host.	☐	☐	☐
Whenever I visit a company, I expect the host to initiate all the small talk.	☐	☐	☐

Study focus

When business visitors arrive, it is your job as host to put them at ease. You can do this in many ways: by helping them to prepare for their trip, for example, but also by making small talk with them. As a guest, it is your job to show that you appreciate what your host has done for you and to make small talk. This way, both the host and guest feel comfortable about taking steps to do business together.

Key phrases

As a host: Welcoming words
Welcome to Qatar/our head office.
How was your trip/flight?
(It's) great/good to see you here. / Is this your first time here?
Did you have any problems finding us?
How was the weather in Berlin?

As a host: Offering food, drink and help
Let me help you with your case/bag/luggage.
Can I take your coat? / Can I get you anything?
Can I offer you something to drink? Coffee, tea, water?
Please help yourselves to the sandwiches/snacks.
You must be hungry/thirsty/tired/jet-lagged after your flight.
If there's anything you need, please just ask.

As a host: Responding to thanks
No problem. / My pleasure. / You're welcome.
I'm glad to hear that.

As a guest: Showing appreciation and interest
It's good to be here. / It's great to see you again.
The flight was fine/bumpy. I'm glad to be back on the ground.
Thank you for picking me up/making the hotel arrangements.
Your directions were great/really helpful/clear.

As a guest: Accepting food, drink and help
Thank you. That's very kind of you.

As a guest: Travel small talk
How far is it to the office?

 Go to www.collinselt.com/businessresources
to listen to the key phrases.

Scenarios

Milena: **Welcome to our office. Good to see you here.**

Alex: **It's good to be here.**

Milena: **How was the trip?** You drove from Munich, right?

Alex: Yes, and **the trip was fine. Your directions were great.**

Milena: Terrific! **Now, can I offer you something to drink? Tea? Coffee?**

Alex: Coffee, please. Black.

Juan: **Welcome to Barcelona. How was your flight?**

Katerina: Very pleasant. **Thank you for picking me up.**

Juan: **My pleasure. Let me help you with your luggage.**

Katerina: **Oh, thank you. That's very kind of you.**

Juan: **So, you must be jet-lagged after your flight.**

Katerina: Not really. I managed to sleep. There weren't any screaming babies on the flight.

Juan: Wow, that must be a first!

Katerina: I know. I couldn't believe my luck.

Roberto: **Is this your first time in Rio,** Rebecca?

Rebecca: No, I was here in 2010. For a conference.

Roberto: So you know the city.

Rebecca: I do, actually, quite well. It's a beautiful city.

Roberto: **How was the weather in Warsaw?**

Rebecca: Wet and grey.

Roberto: Well, it'll be hot and sunny today.

Rebecca: Excellent!

 Go to www.collinselt.com/businessresources
to listen to the scenarios.

Over to you

1 What can you say to make an offer? Complete the words in the sentences.

1 Can I t _ _ _ your coat?

2 Can I g _ _ you anything?

3 Can I o _ _ _ _ you something to drink?

4 Can I p _ _ _ you up from the airport?

5 Can I h _ _ _ you with anything?

2 What can you say to find out how your guest is feeling? Re-arrange the letters in brackets and complete the sentences.

1 You must be .... (thystir)

2 You must be .... (redit)

3 You must be .... (tej-ladegg)

4 You must be .... (gurhny)

3 Put the dialogue in the correct order.

.... **Nina:** My pleasure. It's very cold outside. Are you ready?

.... **Nina:** Well, don't expect to see much sun here during your trip.

.... **Nina:** You must be tired.

.... **Nina:** You'll need it. How was the weather in Sydney when you left?

.... **Nina:** Welcome to Kiev. How was your flight?

.... **Jules:** Yes, I am. I bought a new coat for this trip!

.... **Jules:** Beautiful. Very sunny!

.... **Jules:** I won't. So, how far is it to your office?

.... **Jules:** No, I'm fine. I slept the whole trip. Thank you for picking me up, by the way.

.... **Jules:** Very long. I'm glad to be back on the ground.

4 **Complete the dialogues.**

1 **A:** Thank you for picking me up.

　　B: My ....

2 **A:** Thank you for making the hotel arrangements.

　　B: No ....

3 **A:** It's good to be here.

　　B: It's great ....

4 **A:** Thank you for the directions. They were really clear.

　　B: I'm glad ....

5 **What can a good host say? Use the words to make sentences.**

1 help / you / luggage

....

2 please / help / sandwiches

....

3 anything / you / need / ask

....

4 offer / something / drink

....

6 **Complete the dialogue.**

Carla: Welcome to Peru. It's good to see you here.

　You: **(1)** *(Answer with enthusiasm.)*

....

Carla: How was your flight?

　You: **(2)** *(Answer and then ask about the weather.)*

....

Carla: It's pretty hot, actually. About 35 degrees.

　You: **(3)** *(Answer that it is OK because you have your sunglasses.)*

....

Remember this! Time and dress code

Time

Attitudes to time vary across cultures. What are your own attitudes? Are you usually on time? Do people who are late make you angry? Do you expect meetings to start and finish on time?

What do you know about the attitudes of the people you are visiting? Can you find out? In India, for example, people may be more relaxed about time than people in the US or northern Europe. Meetings and appointments may not happen at the agreed time. However, many companies are run according to Western time-keeping traditions, so be prepared to be on time. You will learn the general rules when you spend time with your business contacts.

What is the best advice for dealing with different attitudes to time? Be flexible – bring something to read in case you *do* have to wait. And be patient!

Dress code

If you are wearing clothes that are similar to what your hosts are wearing, you will feel more at ease. Read up about the culture that you are visiting. There are lots of helpful books about cultural differences, or try the internet. You could also ask business contacts in your host country what is appropriate. For example, women might be expected to wear a headscarf if they are visiting conservative Muslim countries.

Andy: *This is my first trip to Mumbai. What should I wear? Do people wear suits in your office?*

Rohan: *Everyone wears a jacket and tie. It's hot outside at this time of year, but offices are air-conditioned.*

Andy: *Thanks, Rohan. That's good to know.*

Tips: Travel small talk

- It might be appropriate to make small talk with your fellow travellers. Here are some useful phrases you could use.
  Looks like we're in for some turbulence/bad weather/delays.
  Are you flying on to somewhere else?
  Is this your first time to Kyoto?

- Be careful: many people don't like to talk when they are travelling. If you are getting one-word replies, this is a sure sign that your fellow traveller just wants some peace and quiet.

Language focus: International travel

Here is some useful vocabulary for when you have business visitors or when you are travelling internationally yourself.

- **boarding pass:** *I downloaded my boarding pass onto my phone.*

- **cancel:** *All flights out of Gatwick have been cancelled.*

- **connecting flight:** *My flight to Frankfurt was delayed, so I almost missed my connecting flight.*

- **customs:** *It took quite a while to go through customs since I had some product samples with me.*

- **declare:** *I had to declare my samples at customs.*

- **delay:** *My flight was delayed by almost an hour.*

- **flight number:** *I'll pick you up at the airport. What's your flight number?*

- **hand luggage/carry-on luggage:** *I only have hand luggage.*

- **layover:** *Singapore is a great place for a layover.*

- **return flight:** *My return flight isn't until 11 p.m.*

- **security:** *Since I checked in online and I don't have any luggage, I can go straight through to security.*

- **suit bag/garment bag:** *I had to check in my suit bag and it hasn't arrived!*

- **travel light:** *I always travel light so I don't have to check any luggage in at the airport.*

Next steps

For hosts

Most business travellers don't have time to visit places of interest, but that doesn't mean they aren't interested in them. Make sure you know how to describe the main tourist sights to people who visit your town, city or country.

- Get a tourist map or download a tourist app to your smartphone and look up the places of interest in your area.

- Make sure you can describe some of them in a few short sentences.

- If possible, find out something interesting, strange or funny to say about the main places.

- Tell your guest about important local companies and their products too. The companies don't have to be in the same industry, but your guest may like to learn about your local economy and what types of businesses are important for the area.

- If there is time, you could also tell them about other foreign companies that are based in the area – or about local companies that have offices in your guest's country. Making a reference to your guest's country will show that you are interested in their situation too.

Start with something that people might see when they are travelling from the airport or train station to your office. If you pick them up from the airport, you can mention the places you pass on the drive. Most visitors will thank you for the information and for making the extra effort.

For guests

As a guest, you could prepare yourself for a trip by doing the same. You should try to learn how to pronounce the names of places in the local language as well as 'thank you'. You will please your host.

 Go to www.collinselt.com/businessresources to listen to the real-life audio for this chapter.

My goals
- Make a personal connection
- Talk about personal and family matters
- Deepen relationships

Quiz

Ask yourself: 'Am I able to share and exchange personal details in small talk?'

	Absolutely	Sometimes	No, I don't
I avoid telling people about my family.	☐	☐	☐
I like to remember details about people so I can refer to them in the future.	☐	☐	☐
I find it helps to build a personal connection with someone when I learn about their background.	☐	☐	☐
I think that asking a lot of questions about someone's family and background can cause problems.	☐	☐	☐
I prefer to keep personal information private and to focus on business only.	☐	☐	☐

Study focus

Using small talk to exchange personal information is an essential part of the process of getting to know someone better. If you remember the details that people share with you, you can refer to them the next time you communicate. This will show that you care about a person as an individual rather than just as a business acquaintance and will help to deepen a relationship.

Key phrases

Volunteering information
I was born here/there. / I grew up here/there.
I'm originally from London, but I live in Rome now.
My wife/husband/partner is from Kiev.
My daughter got engaged/got married/turned fifteen last year.

Follow-up questions and comments
How many children do you have?
Oh, you have a daughter! How old is she?
How are the children doing? / How is everyone?
How did the move to Madrid/the suburbs go?
What language(s) do you speak at home?

Checking what you think you know
Didn't your daughter move to Shanghai?
Aren't you originally from Rome?
I hear you speak three languages. Is that right?
How did you end up in Russia?

Showing appreciation
It's very good of you to remember. Thanks for asking.
You have a very good memory. It's kind of you to ask.

Responding to good news
(That's) really wonderful/really fascinating. / How nice/funny!
Oh, lovely/wonderful! You must be very proud.
Congratulations! / That's wonderful news!

Responding to bad news
That must be tough/hard/difficult.
How awful/terrible/sad! I'm so sorry to hear that.

 Go to www.collinselt.com/businessresources
to listen to the key phrases.

Scenarios

Sara: I hear you speak three languages. Is that right?

Giovanni: Yes. **My mother is from Rome**, so she spoke Italian to us at home. My father spoke English and Hindi – he was from India. So **I grew up in New York** speaking Italian, English and Hindi.

Sara: Fascinating. What language do you speak with your partner at home? Isn't she Spanish?

Giovanni: Well, …

Filipe: How did the move go?

Andrew: It went very well. **Thanks for asking.**

Filipe: And the children? **How are they doing?**

Andrew: Fine. We've lived here in Hamburg before, when I first started working for the company, but the children were very young at the time.

Filipe: How old are they now?

Andrew: Paul is nearly sixteen and my daughter will be 23 next month. **She just got engaged.**

Filipe: **Oh, that's wonderful news! Congratulations!** When's the big day?

Andrew: They haven't decided yet. I'm hoping they'll wait a few years. 23 is very young to get married, I think.

Filipe: Oh, I don't know. I was only 20 when I got married. The first time ...

 Go to www.collinselt.com/businessresources to listen to the scenarios.

Over to you

1 **Choose the correct word.**

1 How **old / young** is your son?

2 How **do / did** you end up in London?

3 How **many / much** children do you have?

4 How is **anyone / everyone**?

2 **Write questions using the words in brackets.**

1 **A:** .... (born / Paris)

   B: No, in London, actually.

2 **A:** .... (originally / from Chennai)

   B: No, I'm from Delhi.

3 **A:** .... (end / Berlin)

   B: My wife is German and we decided to move here in 2008.

4 **A:** .... (grow / France)

   B: Yes, I did. In Besançon.

5 **A:** .... (always / live / here)

   B: No, I've lived in many different countries.

3 **Write the words in the correct group.**

anniversary	divorced	married	uncle
birthday	engaged	mother-in-law	wedding
cousin	fiancé	spouse	wife
daughter	grandchild	step-child	

Marital status	Partners	Special occasions	Relatives
single	husband	honeymoon	father-in-law

4 **What can you ask to check if you have remembered personal information correctly? Put the words in the correct order. Don't forget to add punctuation.**

1 or / that / girls / is / it / two / you / three / have

....

2 your / isn't / Berlin / studying / in / daughter

....

3 you / just / haven't / moved

....

4 you / big / don't / dog / have / a

....

5 am / thinking / you / grew / I / in / Malta / right / up / in

....

5 **What can you say to show that you appreciate that someone has asked you something about your family or background? Complete the words in the sentences.**

1 It's very good of you to r _ _ _ _ _ _ _ .

2 Thanks for a _ _ _ _ _ .

3 You have a very good m _ _ _ _ _ .

4 It's very k _ _ _ of you to ask.

6 **Choose three of the topics and write a short description of yourself.**

birthday	birthplace	children	growing up
languages	moving	pets	

1 ....

....

2 ....

....

3 ....

....

Remember this! Avoiding stereotypes

We are all individuals

We are all individuals, no matter what culture we come from. So when you are working with people from other cultures, it is important to avoid stereotyping them; this is dangerous and can lead you to think that you know something about someone when you don't. Get to know the people you meet as individuals. They may surprise you. In many countries, particularly China, Russia and India, attitudes to traditional values are changing very fast.

Family values

There are also stereotypes about family values. In the US, Canada and many northern European cultures, families are often thought of as small. In these countries you will also often come across so-called 'patchwork' families, in which the parents may have got divorced and remarried (maybe more than once) and have children with different partners. Some children may be adopted. There may be one-parent families and unmarried or gay couples. It can be complicated.

In other cultures, families can often seem much bigger. The extended family is important and may include many cousins, uncles, aunts and more distant relatives.

Family business

Families may play an important role in business, particularly when a company is new. However, international companies can also be run by a family. When you make small talk about families, you could learn something important about the structure or history of a company. Here are examples of the kinds of things you might hear.

My great-grandfather founded the business in 1920.
The company has been in the family since 1886.
My father-in-law is in charge of production.
My boss retires next year and his son will run the business.
It's a small, family-owned business.

Tips: Being sensitive

It is best not to ask directly if someone has children or is married. Listen out for details that a person tells you and ask follow-up questions in a sensitive way. Here are two examples.

John: I have to get back. It's my daughter's birthday tomorrow.

George: Oh, you have a daughter! How old will she be?

Bert: I just won this gadget at the ABC stand.

Alexia: It's pretty cool.

Bert: Isn't it? But I bet my son will steal it from me when I get home.

Alexia: Oh, you have a son! How old is he?

Bert: He's fifteen and loves technology.

Alexia: Tell me about it! My daughter already knows more than me – and I'm a programmer.

Bert: How funny!

If you feel people are starting to ask too many personal questions, bring the topic back to business. For example, in the dialogue between Alexia and Bert above, Alexia could change the topic to a less personal one.

Alexia: Are you programming anything interesting at the moment?

Bert: I am, actually.

Next steps

When you learn a word, it is a good idea to also learn words that are made from the same word or that are connected. Look at the 'word family' below and how you can use the words in different situations and in different combinations.

relate	related	unrelated
relative	relatively	close relative
distant relative	relationship	relations

Family matters
*We're not **related**, but we have the same last name.*
*I have **relatives** in Ireland.*
*I have a **distant relative** in South Africa.*
*The wedding was small – we only invited **close relatives**.*
*My children have a **good relationship**. They're very close.*

Business matters
*On a **related matter**, can I ask you something about the venue?*
*On a totally **unrelated topic**, can I ask you about the system you use?*
*You need small talk to build a **good working relationship**.*
*We're **relatively new** to this event. It's only the second time that we've been to it.*
*There's been a great improvement in **relations** between the two departments.*

Create your own 'word families' when you learn new words. Don't forget to make sentences using the words as this will help you to remember them. Here is a suggestion to get you started.

employ	employment	employer	employed	unemployed

 Go to www.collinselt.com/businessresources to listen to the real-life audio for this chapter.

8 Using everyday moments

My goals
- Recognize small talk opportunities at work
- Become more confident about introducing small talk topics
- Make appropriate comments and compliments

Quiz

Ask yourself: 'How good am I at making the most of small talk opportunities?'

	Absolutely	Sometimes	No, I don't
I prefer to sit in silence rather than try to find something to talk about.	☐	☐	☐
I feel that some people are much better than I am at talking informally.	☐	☐	☐
I know when it's a good time to make a personal comment.	☐	☐	☐
I listen carefully so that I can use opportunities to make small talk.	☐	☐	☐
I avoid making compliments because people might misunderstand my intentions.	☐	☐	☐

Study focus

Small talk isn't only about building relationships with external partners and clients. It is also about building relationships with people who work at the same company as you. Ask your colleagues about their weekend or what their hobbies are while making a cup of coffee. Notice personal things on people's desks and comment on them. Tell people something about your life outside work.

Key phrases

Kick-starting small talk

Did you have a good weekend? / How was your weekend?
What are your plans for the festive season?
I see your team won/lost/played last night.
That's a lovely/an unusual photo. Where was it taken?
That's a lovely/an unusual painting. Where was it painted?
I hear/understand you sail/you're into sailing. Is that right?

Sharing information about yourself

I'm going to the theatre/cinema tonight.
I saw a great play/movie last night/on Saturday.
I (don't) really enjoy sports. / I'm (not) really into sports.

Using follow-up questions or comments

(Are) you doing anything special this weekend?
(Have you got) anything planned/any plans for tonight?
How often do you go to concerts? / (Do you) go to concerts a lot?
Are you into sports at all? / Do you get much time to do sports?
(Have you) read any good books/seen any good movies lately?
(Was it) any good? / What did you think of it? / And?

Finding a connection

What about you? / Really? That's a coincidence! I also …
(No way!) So am/do/did/have I. /
(No way!) Me too. / (No way!) I am as well.
Me neither. / Neither am/do/did/have I.
I'm more of a pop fan/movie fan myself.
I've never tried it/done it myself (but I'd like to).
I've never been there myself (but I'd like to go).
I'm not really into sports/movies, but I read a lot/enjoy music.

 Go to www.collinselt.com/businessresources
to listen to the key phrases.

Scenarios

Ruth:	**That's a lovely photo. Where was it taken?**
Min:	In Thailand. I was there last year with my family.
Ruth:	It's beautiful. You have a very good eye!
Min:	Thank you. But it's easy to take good photos there.
Ruth:	**Do you go there a lot?**
Min:	Yes, we do. **My wife and I are into diving** and Thailand's a perfect place for it.
Ruth:	**I've never tried it myself, but I'd like to.**

Leandro:	**Any plans for tonight?**
Marion:	Yes, **we're going to a concert tonight** in town.
Leandro:	Classical or pop?
Marion:	Classical. I used to play the violin and I try to go to a concert once a month.
Leandro:	**I'm more of a pop fan myself.** I played the drums in a band at college.
Marion:	**No way!** Like Ringo Starr?
Leandro:	I'm not that old! And our band was terrible.

Niki:	**Did you have a good weekend, Pauline?**
Pauline:	Pretty good. I ran a marathon on Sunday.
Niki:	Really? Well done! **How often do you run?**
Pauline:	Most days. **Are you into sports at all?**
Niki:	**Well, I'm more of a reader myself.**
Pauline:	**Oh, have you read any good books lately?** I listen to audio books while I run.
Niki:	I've just finished Amy Tan's latest novel. The audio book must be at least 20 hours long.
Pauline:	Long enough for five marathons!

 Go to www.collinselt.com/businessresources to listen to the scenarios.

Over to you

1 **Put the dialogue in the correct order.**

.... **Mette:** How was your weekend, Beth?

.... **Mette:** Now that's a good system. I'll have to suggest it to my husband.

.... **Mette:** You did? What did you think of it?

.... **Mette:** Me too. I love his rom-coms, but my husband hates them.

.... **Beth:** Mine too, but he chose the last movie we went to.

.... **Beth:** Great, thanks. I finally got to see that movie with Tom Hanks that everyone's been talking about.

.... **Beth:** Oh, it was long – but good. I like Tom Hanks.

2 **Put the words in the correct order to make the questions. Don't forget to add punctuation.**

1 golf / time / do / get / much / to / you / play

   A: ....

   B: Not really. I love golf, but most weekends my children have football matches – and I have to watch.

2 was / vacation / your / how

   A: ....

   B: Brilliant! We went to California and drove along the coast from north to south.

3 for / got / you / season / any / the / plans / have / festive

   A: ....

   B: Not really. I think we'll just spend some time at home relaxing.

4 interesting / you / any / read / lately / books / have

   A: ....

   B: Yes, I've just finished a fascinating book about Scott's journey across Antarctica.

5 you / how / go / do / often / swimming

   A: ....

   B: As often as I can. Every weekend in the summer, in fact.

3 Shorten the different possible follow-up questions and comments to make them sound more informal and friendly.

1 **A:** Actually, it's my birthday on Sunday.

   B: Oh, nice. Are you going anywhere special?

   ....

   B: Oh, nice. Do you have any plans?

   ....

2 **A:** I saw the Tom Cruise movie last night.

   B: You did? Was it any good?

   ....

   B: You did? I saw it too.

   ....

4 What can you say to show that you have (or don't have) something in common? Complete the dialogues with the words in the box.

more	neither	to	too	well

1 **A:** My daughter likes playing squash.   **B:** Mine ....

2 **A:** I'm not really into sports.   **B:** Me ....

3 **A:** I love watching old movies.   **B:** I do as ....

4 **A:** I enjoy reading crime stories.   **B:** I'm .... of a sci-fi fan myself.

5 **A:** I go diving at weekends.   **B:** I've never tried it myself, but I'd like ....

5 Write short responses to the questions about you.

1 **A:** What do you do to relax?

   B: Well, I like to ....

2 **A:** Are you into sports at all?

   B: Yes, I am. I enjoy ....

3 **A:** What did you do at the weekend?

   B: ....

4 **A:** Any plans this weekend?

   B: ....

Language focus: Compliments

Paying compliments

Compliments can be a good way to start a conversation.
Typical adjectives used in compliments are 'well', 'cool',
'nice', 'good', 'great', 'lovely', 'unusual' and 'beautiful'.

> *You're looking well. Have you been on holiday?*
> *Great photo. You have a very good eye.*

People may also compliment other people's clothes or possessions.
They may use the verbs 'like' and 'love'.

> *I really like your coat.*
> *I couldn't help noticing your pen. It's really nice.*
> *Hey, cool handbag.*
> *What lovely shoes!*

Responding to compliments

You can respond to a compliment by simply saying 'Thank you'.
You could also make a comment to signal that you are happy to
continue talking about the topic.

> *Thank you. It's nice of you to say so.*
> *Thanks. I bought it in Paris last week.*

If people feel uncomfortable about a compliment, they may try to
'play it down'. This signals that they probably don't want to discuss
it any more.

> *A: Nice tie.*
> *B: Oh, this old thing?*

Be careful when complimenting people of the opposite sex as it may
be taken the wrong way. In some cultures people are more careful
with their compliments. In the Arab world elaborate compliments
are more common. Sometimes, if you make a compliment while
visiting another country, you may find that your business partner
gives you the thing you complimented as a gift. So be careful!

Remember this! Finding common ground

Find the right moment to make a connection by listening out for clues that show that a person is happy to make small talk. If they mention a holiday or an interest, try to follow up on the information they share with you. Even if the exchange lasts only a few minutes, it can make people feel happy to work with you.

Small talk is all about trying to find something you have in common with other people. If you hit on a topic that you are both interested in, you are on your way to creating a good relationship – both working and personal. When you ask people questions, watch their face to see how they react. If their eyes light up or they smile, you have found a hot topic. Which of the topics below would you like to talk about?

current affairs	entertainment	the environment	local events
movies	music	news	sports
tourism	travel	work	

Try to prepare sentences that can help you to talk about your favourite sport or a movie you have recently seen. Don't try to memorize everything, but have an idea of what you would like to say. If the topic is introduced, you will be able to talk about it more easily and with confidence.

As you get to know colleagues, try to remember things about them, such as their interest in movies, sports or music. Whenever possible, try to connect to what people tell you. For example, when someone says, 'I'm going to Dubai for the holidays', you could connect in several ways.

No way! I have a really good friend who's just moved there.
I've always wanted to go there.
What's the weather like there at this time of the year?

Next steps

Vocabulary building

Use 'word maps' to help you to learn vocabulary for different small talk topics. Write the topic in the middle of a blank piece of paper and add words and expressions that you would like to use. This will help you to learn vocabulary related to the topic or area. Here are two examples of topics and useful words and expressions.

- **Music:** album, the blues, classical, the eighties, pop, soul, play an instrument, concert, download a track, stream, subscribe to a music streaming service

- **Movies:** action movie, chick flick, comedy, rom-com, thriller, blockbuster, box office movie, independent movie, low-budget movie, great plot, soundtrack, special effects, Hollywood ending, surprise ending

Verbs and verb forms

It is important to learn which verbs and expressions are typically used to talk about your interests, together with the correct verb structures. Listen to your business partners and make a note of expressions that you could use. Make a list of your own interests using the following structures.

enjoy + noun/-ing form:	*I enjoy reading.*
like/love + noun/-ing form:	*I love (playing) chess.*
be really into + noun/-ing form:	*I'm really into sailing.*
go + -ing form (for an activity):	*I go horse-riding every week.*
play + noun (for a game):	*I play tennis/football/rugby.*
do + noun (for a physical activity):	*I do yoga/Pilates.*

You can talk about your interests in other ways too.
I run marathons.
I compete in races.
I work out in a gym.

 Go to www.collinselt.com/businessresources to listen to the real-life audio for this chapter.

9

Who's who and what's what

My goals
- Introduce a visitor to colleagues
- Give a company tour
- Show interest in how my business partner works

Quiz

Ask yourself: 'Do I use small talk to share information about my company?'

	Absolutely	Sometimes	No, I don't
I know how to describe my company structure to visitors.	☐	☐	☐
I can give a company tour.	☐	☐	☐
I introduce business visitors to colleagues in a way that recommends their skills.	☐	☐	☐
I believe it's useful to know something about your business partner's work day.	☐	☐	☐
I know how to show interest during a company tour.	☐	☐	☐

Study focus

As you get to know your business partners, you will want to share information on how you do business. You might also have to give them a company tour or introduce them to your colleagues. Exchanging information on how you work helps everyone to understand what kind of pressures both parties are under and deepens understanding.

Key phrases

Introducing colleagues and explaining the company structure

I'd like to/Let me introduce you to the team/John/the CEO.

Joe, this is Sue. She's involved in/She's in charge of/She's responsible for Sales.

Come and meet Tom. He's our Sales Manager/agent in Brussels. / He deals with/He takes care of customer complaints.
He heads up/He works for/He runs Finance.

Have you met Jane/everyone (else)?

Let me explain how our organization works.

Company tour

Let me give you a tour of our department/head office/factory.

This is the main building/conference room/canteen/café.

Accounts are on the top floor. The view from there is amazing.

It's a great location. / The facilities are fantastic.

The work day

We have open-plan offices.

Most people work from home one day a week.

Understanding the layout and structure

How does it work here? / How many people work here?

Who's in charge of Marketing/R&D/Production?

Positive comments and requests

What a lovely office/cool building/spectacular view!

You're lucky to have a canteen/fitness centre in the building.

How interesting/convenient! / That's good to know.

It was good to meet your colleagues.

Could I wash my hands/freshen up? / Where's the restroom?

Thank you for giving me a tour/showing me around.

 Go to www.collinselt.com/businessresources
to listen to the key phrases.

Scenarios

Jasmine:	So, Alex, **this is our café.** We'll have lunch here.
Alex:	**You're lucky to have a canteen in the building.**
Jasmine:	Yes, we are. There's usually a great selection of meals. Oh! There's Jill Peterson. **Have you met her? She's in charge of Accounts.**
Alex:	No, I don't think I have.
Jasmine:	**Jill, come and meet Alex, our agent in Athens. Alex, this is Jill Peterson.**
Alex:	Nice to meet you, Jill.
Jill:	Nice to meet you too, Alex.

Lee:	It's great that we could have lunch together before the meeting.
Noor:	The food was really good. **And it was good to meet your colleagues.** By the way, is that Pat over there?
Lee:	That's right. She'll be at our meeting this afternoon.
Noor:	**Isn't she responsible for Production?**
Lee:	She was. **Now she runs the European division.**
Noor:	**That's good to know.**

Sam:	**What a lovely office! The view is spectacular!**
Heidi:	Isn't it? I never get tired of looking at it.
Sam:	I can see why.
Heidi:	We'll go to the conference room in a few minutes.
Sam:	**Could I freshen up first?**
Heidi:	Of course. The restroom's opposite my office.

 Go to www.collinselt.com/businessresources to listen to the scenarios.

Over to you

1 What can you say to make introductions? Put the words in the correct order. Don't forget to add punctuation.

1 introduce / team / me / to / let / you / the

....

2 me / give / let / of / tour / our / a / offices / you

....

3 Andy / meet / come / and

....

4 you / else / have / everyone / met

....

5 like / CEO / to / to / I'd / introduce / you / the

....

6 me / let / organization / works / explain / our / how

....

2 Choose the correct word.

1 John heads **up / off** Marketing.

2 Rob is **of / in** charge of Sales.

3 Markus works **up / for** our French company.

4 Marissa deals **for / with** customer complaints.

5 Suki takes care **of / in** the production schedule.

6 I'm responsible **for / with** project management.

3 What can you say when you give a company tour? Complete the sentences with the words in the box.

building   canteen   conference   floor   location   open-plan

1 We're having a meeting in the .... room later.

2 Your head office is in an amazing ....

3 This is the main .... It's over 100 years old.

4 We have .... offices so it can be quite noisy.

5 We're on the twenty-first ....

6 The .... serves food all day until 8 p.m.

4 **Complete the words in the positive comments.**

1 What a **spect** _ _ _ _ _ _ view!

2 You're very **l** _ _ _ _ to have a fitness centre!

3 What a **c** _ _ _ building!

4 How **int** _ _ _ _ _ _ _ _ !

5 How **conv** _ _ _ _ _ _ !

6 That's **g** _ _ **d** to know.

7 Thank you for showing me **ar** _ _ _ _ .

5 **Complete the questions with the words in the box.**

could	how	how many	where	who

1 ....'s in charge of Marketing?

2 .... does it work here?

3 ....'s the restroom?

4 .... I freshen up before the meeting?

5 .... people work here?

6 **Complete the dialogue.**

John: Thank you for giving me a tour.

You: **(1)** *(Tell your visitor something about your offices.)*

....

John: So, will the whole team be at the meeting this afternoon?

You: **(2)** *(Name three people who will be at the meeting and explain what they do in your organization.)*

....

....

....

John: That's interesting. Could I ask who's in charge of Marketing?

You: **(3)** *(Explain how things work in your company.)*

....

John: Thanks. That's good to know.

Tip: Structuring small talk

The better you structure your small talk, the more successful it will be. Try to follow this structure to get the most out of it.

Question → Answer → Comment/Question → Answer/Question

Paul:	Where do you normally have lunch? *(Question)*
Julienne:	We share a canteen with another company. It's on the ground floor. *(Answer)*
Paul:	How convenient! Is the food any good? *(Comment/Question)*
Julienne:	Most of the time, yes. I'm a vegetarian, so sometimes it's hard to find something that I can eat. What do you normally do for lunch? *(Answer/Question)*

Language focus: Recommending colleagues

In business you often need to recommend a colleague to your business partner. When you do this, mention anything about your colleague's background or experience that is relevant.

He has an MBA/a law degree from Harvard.
He has a lot of experience in production.
She's lived in Asia and speaks Mandarin Chinese.
She studied international relations/politics/chemistry.

If you make small talk about other people in a company, keep it professional, positive and neutral.

John will answer your questions about the software update. He's the one with a degree in engineering from Imperial.
Sarah has a lot of experience in e-learning. She'll explain the system to you later.
Marion lived in Asia for years, so she knows the market well.

Remember this! Corporate culture

It is a good idea to try to understand what your business partner's work day is like and the pressures they are under. You might find it useful to ask the following questions.

How flexible is your working day?
When do you normally start/finish work?
Do you ever work from home?
Do you ever discuss business during social events?

Giving and receiving gifts

Some companies, particularly in the US, UK and Germany, have strict policies about gifts. Employees aren't allowed to give or accept gifts above a certain value. If the gift is clearly above this value, you may hear the following.

It's so nice of you, but I'm sorry, I can't accept it. It's company policy, I'm afraid.
I really appreciate it, but I can't accept it.

In Japan don't give a gift to just one person. If you take gifts, bring something for the team, such as a box of chocolates. In the UK and the US people often protest a little when they receive a gift. After saying 'Thank you so much', you might add 'You really shouldn't have'. People do the same in Japan as well.

In Japan and China most people don't unwrap a gift in front of others. If you aren't sure what to do, you could say 'Thank you. Should I open it now?' Your host will let you know what to do.

In Germany it is important to take flowers with you if you are invited to someone's home. In the UK people often take a box of chocolates or flowers. In China people like to give flowers, but don't give red or white flowers or a quantity of four flowers; this is considered unlucky.

Next steps

Here is some useful vocabulary for talking about your company and understanding how other companies work. Write an example sentence for each expression that you think will be useful.

- **Accounts:** the department that deals with financial records
- **Customer Services:** the department that deals with customers
- **customer:** a person who buys a product or service
- **Head of Marketing:** the person in charge of marketing
- **Marketing:** the department that deals with promoting products and services
- **Production:** the department that deals with the manufacturing process
- **Sales Manager:** the person who is responsible for selling a company's products or services
- **Sales:** the department that deals with selling products and services

Corporate abbreviations

Many companies use abbreviations or short forms. Here are some common ones that are used internationally.

- *The company encourages **BYOD**.* (bring your own device)
- *The **CEO** is from France.* (Chief Executive Officer)
- *The **CFO** speaks five languages.* (Chief Financial Officer)
- ***HR** is investing more in training.* (Human Resources)
- *John works in **IT**.* (Information Technology)
- *I worked for an **NGO** in Africa.* (non-government organization)
- *We spend a lot on **PR**.* (Public Relations)
- *We invest a lot in **R&D**.* (Research and Development)
- *We work with a number of **SMEs**.* (small and medium-sized enterprises (i.e. small or medium-sized companies))

 Go to www.collinselt.com/businessresources to listen to the real-life audio for this chapter.

10

Entertaining

My goals
- Entertain and be entertained
- Make and accept invitations
- Feel confident about making small talk in a restaurant

Quiz

Ask yourself: 'How comfortable am I when I eat out with international business partners?'

	Absolutely	Sometimes	No, I don't
I know how to talk about food and drink at a business event.	☐	☐	☐
I ask whether people have food preferences or allergies before I invite them out.	☐	☐	☐
I know how to check that guests are enjoying their meal.	☐	☐	☐
I feel uncomfortable in situations when I don't understand what's in the food.	☐	☐	☐
I try to compliment the host's choice of food and drink.	☐	☐	☐

Study focus

Enjoying a meal in a group is a shared experience that can bring people together. If your business contacts invite you to lunch or dinner, it is an opportunity to get to know them better. Some business contacts may want to conduct business over the meal, so be prepared. In many cases the host might order the food for everyone, often choosing a local speciality for you to try.

Key phrases

Inviting someone for a meal

Would you like to join me for dinner this evening?
Can you stay for lunch? / Can we take you out for dinner?

Accepting or declining an invitation

Thank you. I'd love to. / That would be nice/great. /
I'd like that very much. / (That) sounds perfect/great (to me).
That would be nice, but I'm afraid I can't.
I'd love to, but I fly back tonight/I've already made plans.

Talking about food allergies or preferences

Is there anything I need to know before I make a reservation?
Is there anything you can't eat? / Are you allergic to anything?
I don't drink alcohol. / I don't eat pork/shellfish/beef.
I'm a (strict) vegan/vegetarian. / I eat everything.

Talking about the meal

Do you need any help with the menu?
Would you like a dessert/something else/some more wine?
It's delicious/spicy/mild. / It's like ... / It contains ...
Can you recommend something (else)?
What's in it? / What are the main ingredients?
How's your main course/dessert?
You should try the vegetables/rice/cheesecake/sauce.

Making and receiving compliments

This wine is crisp/delicious/fruity. / The meat is juicy/tender.
It was fabulous, but I couldn't possibly eat any more.
Wow! I've never tasted anything quite like this before.
Compliments to the chef!
Thanks for bringing me here. It's been a wonderful experience.
My pleasure. I'm so glad you like the food/the restaurant.

 Go to www.collinselt.com/businessresources
to listen to the key phrases.

Scenarios

Jen:	**Would you like to join us for dinner this evening?**
Paul:	**Thank you. I'd love to.**
Jen:	There's a restaurant near your hotel that serves fantastic local dishes. Do you eat fish?
Paul:	Yes, I do. **Sounds good.**
Jen:	**Is there anything I need to know before I make a reservation? Are you allergic to anything?**
Paul:	No, **I eat everything.** What time shall we say?
Jen:	How about eight? I'll wait for you in the hotel lobby.
Paul:	Perfect.

Mario:	**Can you stay for lunch today?**
Jules:	**Oh, that would be nice, but** I've already planned another meeting on the other side of town. Next time?
Mario:	Definitely. Don't forget.

Sevda:	**How's your main course?** Is everything OK?
Axel:	Yes, perfect! Thank you. **It's delicious. What's in it?**
Sevda:	Lamb, spinach and a selection of spices. **You should also try the rice. It's spicy**, so have some yoghurt with it.
Axel:	**Wow! I've never tasted anything quite like it.**
Sevda:	**I'm so glad you like it.**
Axel:	**Thank you for bringing me here.**
Sevda:	**My pleasure. Would you like some more wine?**
Axel:	Thank you. It's really good, by the way. Very fruity.

 Go to www.collinselt.com/businessresources
to listen to the scenarios.

Over to you

1 What can you ask your business partner? Make questions.

Would you	need any	to anything?
Are you	I need to	help with the menu?
Can we	allergic	something else?
Can you	like to	for lunch today?
Do you	stay	out for lunch?
Could	take you	join us for dinner?
Is there anything	you recommend	know before I make a reservation?

2 What can you say to accept or decline an invitation? Complete the sentences with one word in each gap.

1 I'd .... to.

2 That .... be great.

3 I'd .... that very much.

4 I'm .... I can't.

5 That .... perfect.

3 One word in each sentence is wrong. Find the correct word in one of the other sentences. Rewrite them so they make sense.

1 I've never tasted anything ~~possibly~~ like this before.

   ....

2 ~~Experience~~ to the chef!

   ....

3 The meal was ~~here~~!

   ....

4 Thank you for bringing me ~~fabulous~~.

   ....

5 It's been a wonderful ~~compliments~~.

   ....

6 I couldn't ~~quite~~ eat another thing.

   ....

4 Complete the sentences with the words in the box.

course dessert fruity ingredients spicy vegetarian

1 This is delicious! What are the main ....?

2 I'm a(n) ...., so I don't eat meat or fish.

3 Why don't you have the steak as a main ....?

4 I love the wine. It's really ....!

5 I think I'll have the cheesecake for ....

6 I can't eat the curry, I'm afraid. I don't eat .... food.

5 Put the dialogue in the correct order.

.... **Meg:** Anja, would you like to join us for dinner?

.... **Meg:** How about 7:30? I'll wait for you in the hotel lobby.

.... **Meg:** Not at all. We can go to another restaurant. Is there anything else I need to know before I make a reservation?

.... **Meg:** There's a restaurant just around the corner from your hotel that serves fantastic local dishes. Do you like lamb?

.... **Anja:** No, I eat everything else. What time shall we say?

.... **Anja:** Perfect.

.... **Anja:** I'd like that very much.

.... **Anja:** Actually, I'm a vegetarian. I hope that won't be a problem.

6 Complete the dialogue.

Nadja: Would you like to join us for dinner this evening?

You: **(1)** *(Accept the invitation.)* ....

Nadja: Is there anything I need to know before I make a reservation?

You: **(2)** *(Explain any food allergies or preferences that you have. If you don't have any, say so.)*

....

Nadja: Great. So I'll make a reservation in a restaurant nearby. Should I pick you up at eight in the hotel lobby?

You: **(3)** *(Accept enthusiastically.)* ....

Language focus: Paying the bill

At business events the hosts generally pay the bill (or 'check', if you are in the US). If business partners or colleagues go out for an informal meal, they often 'split the bill', which means they share the bill equally. In the US and the UK this is common. However, in some countries, for example in Germany, people often pay for their own meals. In France the host usually pays the bill.

In informal situations people may even have a friendly argument over the bill, often using idiomatic language.

Paul:	This is my treat.
Georgina:	No, I won't hear of it.
Paul:	Really, I insist. It's on me.
Georgina:	Shall we split it?
Paul:	No, let me get it.
Georgina:	Are you sure?
Paul:	Of course.
Georgina:	Well, thank you. That's very kind of you. But you must let me take care of the next bill!
Paul:	Absolutely.

Refusing food politely

In some countries the host orders food for everyone, so you don't need to worry about understanding the menu. Try to eat whatever you are offered, but if you really can't eat something, you should say so politely. Use 'I think', 'I'm afraid', 'a little' or 'a bit' to soften your comments. Add 'for me' to show that there is nothing wrong with the meal itself, only that the food is different from what you normally eat.

I'm sorry, but I think it's a bit too raw for me.
I'm afraid it's a little too spicy for me.

Use 'Do you mind if I order something else?' or 'Could I order something else?' to ask for another dish.

Thank you, but I'd rather not eat raw fish. Do you mind if I order something else?

Remember this! Entertaining in different cultures

Different cultures have different ideas about what makes an appropriate night out for a business partner, so find out what a typical night out might be like before you make arrangements.

The **British** might invite you to go to the pub straight after work. At the pub you could offer to buy 'a round of drinks', which means that you buy a drink for everyone in the group.

The **Czechs, Danes** and **Germans** like to have direct eye contact when they make a toast by clinking beer or wine glasses. It is considered extremely rude not to look at people.

People in **Mediterranean** countries may spend longer on their lunches or go out for a meal late in the evening, often after nine or ten. It is quite unusual to go out just for a drink.

In **Russia** you will often be invited to drink vodka with business partners. If you accept the invitation, you should drink the vodka shot in one go – don't drink it slowly.

In **India** and the **Arab world**, if you are in a place where people eat with their hands, always use the right hand. The left hand is considered unclean.

In some cultures in **East Asia** it is considered rude to accept food immediately. People wait to be offered several times before they accept. This is especially true in **Indonesia**.

If you are using chopsticks in **China**, never leave them standing up in the rice dish. It reminds people of the burning of incense sticks at funerals.

In **Japan** people like to socialize with business partners. You might be asked to join a group of colleagues at a karaoke bar, where everyone is expected to sing.

Next steps

It is a good idea to revise regularly. Here are some tips to help you to learn better.

- Practise key phrases for ten minutes every day.
- Say the key phrases in different ways: whisper them softly, shout them out loud, sing them, say them slowly, say them fast, say them with enthusiasm!
- Personalize the key phrases by adapting the scenarios. Rewrite them and record them.
- Write down a list of five vocabulary items or key phrases and learn them in that order. Keep adding items to the list until you can't remember all of them in the same order.
- Think about a special meal that you have had. Was it the food that made it special? The guests? The restaurant? What could you say about the meal? Practise until you can talk about it with confidence.

You can learn more restaurant vocabulary by thinking about your food and drink in English. Whenever you eat out in a restaurant, translate the main ingredients of a dish into English. If you don't know the words, make a note of them or look them up in the dictionary on your smartphone if you have one. You can use a smartphone in other ways too.

- Take a picture of a speciality and the description of the speciality on the menu.
- At home look at the pictures and try to write your own description in English.
- Personalize your description by including your reactions to the dish. Think about interesting information you could tell business visitors about it. What are the ingredients? Why is the dish popular? Is it difficult to make at home?

 Go to www.collinselt.com/businessresources to listen to the real-life audio for this chapter.

11 Tell us a story

My goals
- Tell interesting stories
- Use humour in small talk
- Show interest in stories

Quiz

Ask yourself: 'How good a storyteller am I?'

	Absolutely	Sometimes	No, I don't
I enjoy telling stories about the places I've been to and the things I've seen.	☐	☐	☐
I understand how to structure a story so that it's easy for people to follow.	☐	☐	☐
I react well to anecdotes and know how to show interest in stories.	☐	☐	☐
I think it's a bad idea to tell jokes to business partners.	☐	☐	☐
I like to tell jokes in English and I make people laugh.	☐	☐	☐

Study focus

Storytelling is a useful skill. People tell stories to sell their products, to promote their companies and to make small talk. If you can tell a short, amusing story in English, your listeners will be impressed. Humour can help to break tension and reveal a more informal aspect of your personality. Even if your English isn't perfect, your listeners will appreciate that you have tried. It is also important to react appropriately to someone else's story.

Key phrases

Beginning the story

I'll never forget the time I … / I remember the time I … / Did I ever tell you about the time I …

Funny you should say that, but a similar thing happened to me.

It's a few years ago now. / It was back in 1999.

It was before we had mobiles. / Anyway, back then …

Describing the main action or surprise elements

You're not going to believe this, but ..

You'll never guess who/what/why/how …

To top it all, we lost the game.

You should have seen their faces!

And the funny/strange/awful thing was, I got lost.

Signalling the end of the story

Anyway, in the end, … / Anyway, to cut a long story short, …

(It) seems/sounds funny now, but it wasn't at the time.

Making a comment and showing interest

So what happened then/next? / So are you saying that you …?

Lucky you! / That was lucky! / You're lucky that …

Honestly! / Imagine! / I know!

You can't be serious! / You're joking, right? / You're kidding! / I don't believe it!

How strange/terrible/terrifying/funny/amazing/fantastic!

What a nightmare/disaster/story! / That's hilarious/so funny!

I'm not surprised. / That's what I thought.

Were you all right/hurt/OK?

 Go to www.collinselt.com/businessresources to listen to the key phrases.

Scenario

Nisha: So, Sylvia, you said that you had worked in Germany before. Did you enjoy working there?

Sylvia: Yes, I did. **I'll never forget the day** I started my first job in Berlin. **It was back in 1996.**

Nisha: You must have been very young.

Sylvia: I was – fresh out of college and keen to start working. I decided to go to work before eight on my first day, but when I arrived at the office, there was nobody there.

Nisha: Really? I thought the Germans start work really early.

Sylvia: They do, but that morning the office was locked. **This was before we had mobiles**, so I couldn't call anyone. Anyway, I waited and waited. For an hour.

Nisha: **So what happened?**

Sylvia: **You'll never guess.** At 8:45 my new boss turned up. He looked surprised and asked me why I was so early.

Nisha: **How strange!**

Sylvia: **That's what I thought.** I said to him: 'But it's 8:45.' He laughed. And then told me that the clocks had gone back an hour early Sunday morning.

Nisha: **So are you saying that** you had arrived before seven o'clock? **That's so funny!**

Sylvia: **Seems funny now, but it wasn't at the time.** I was so embarrassed!

 Go to www.collinselt.com/businessresources to listen to the scenario.

Over to you

1 What can you say to begin a story? Complete the sentences with the words in the box.

forget	remember	say	tell

1 I .... when I arrived in Tokyo for the first time.

2 Did I ever .... you about the time I missed my flight?

3 Funny you should .... that, but a similar thing happened to me.

4 I'll never .... the time I couldn't get a hotel room in Paris.

2 At which point of a story would you use each sentence? Write …

- … **B** if you would use it to begin a story.
- … **C** if you would use it to describe the context.
- … **S** if you would use it to describe a surprise element.
- … **E** if you would use it to signal the end of the story.

1 And the funny thing was, I had met him before. ....

2 Anyway, to cut a long story short, I came back on my own. ....

3 Did I ever tell you about the time I went to Tokyo? ....

4 I'll never forget the time I got lost on Hydra. ....

5 It was back in 2010. ....

6 It's a few years ago now. ....

7 Seems funny now, but it wasn't at the time. ....

8 You're not going to believe this, but I nearly ended up in prison. ....

3 Re-arrange the letters in brackets and complete the comments.

1 What a .... ! (amenright)

2 I'm not .... (puresirsd)

3 Sounds .... (firetrying)

4 You can't be .... ! (siseuro)

5 I don't .... it! (veilbee)

6 You must be .... ! (nogkij)

7 You're kidding, ... ? (grith)

8 .... you! (kucly)

9 Were you .... ? (thru)

10 So what .... next? (handpeep)

4 **Complete the dialogues with a comment from exercise 3.**

1 **A:** You're not going to believe this, but I woke up in a different hotel room.

   B: ....

2 **A:** Before I went to Japan, I learnt how to bow properly. Well, one day I was introduced to the CEO of a very important company. So he bowed and I bowed, but I bowed a little too enthusiastically and knocked his glasses off!

   B: ....

3 **A:** I lost my skis and fell down to the bottom of the slope.

   B: ....

4 **A:** Anyway, I was so hungry that I made my husband stop for something to eat. I went in and ordered a pizza. We then continued to Ancona to catch the ferry to Patras. Halfway there I realized I'd left my handbag in the restaurant – with the tickets.

   B: ....

5 **Write a short story using the structure below.**

Did I ever tell you about the time I ....

....

....

It was before I ....

....

You're not going to believe this, but ....

....

To top it all, I ....

....

Anyway, in the end, ...

....

Language focus: Past tenses

When you tell a story about something that happened in the past, you need to use the right tenses.

- Use the **past simple** to talk about past actions or states.
  *I first **travelled** across Siberia in 2001.*

- Use the **past continuous** to talk about an action that was in progress in the past, usually to describe the context for a more important event, which is described using the past simple.
  *I **was travelling** through India when I **lost** my passport.*

- Use the **past perfect** to show that an event happened before another event in the past.
  *By the time the police arrived, the guy **had run away**.*

Tips: Structuring your story

- Begin the story clearly. Let people know that you are going to tell a story.

- Give the story some context. Say when it happened and where before you get started on the main story.

- Describe the main action and/or surprise elements. Use an appropriate key phrase to signal to your listeners that these are the important moments.

- Signal that you have reached the end of the story. There is nothing worse than finishing a story to silence because people haven't realized that you have finished.

And remember: good stories are relevant to your work, your culture or your traditions. They might also highlight something you have learnt or an interesting but little-known fact. Not so good stories are irrelevant and/or long and complicated. Also, avoid stories that are just gossip about other people or simply negative, sad or depressing.

Remember this! Jokes and humour

Humour can be universal, but it is also individual. It is an important part of all cultures, but it can be culture-specific. Humour is an important part of small talk because it can help to break tension and make people feel relaxed. However, it doesn't always translate well across cultures. Generally, it is hard to tell jokes well, but it is especially difficult in a foreign language.

- Wordplay is important for a lot of jokes, and these can be difficult to understand – or make – in a foreign language.

- Many jokes make cultural references that people who are unfamiliar with the culture won't understand. But if the jokes are short, they can be a good way to explain traditions or cultural norms.

- Jokes that need to be explained are no longer funny and may end up creating an embarrassing situation.

- Rude jokes are risky.

- Racist or sexist jokes and stories are not appropriate.

To understand just how hard it is to translate jokes into another language, watch a comedy show in English with the subtitles in your own language. When the audience laugh, do the subtitles make you laugh too? Even the best translators have trouble translating jokes, so be careful when you try to tell one.

Different cultures, different humour

The success of a TV show or movie may be an indication of the type of humour that works well in a particular culture. Slapstick comedy often works across all cultures even when you can't understand a single word. If you work in a multinational company, ask your colleagues what comedy shows they watch. What do they find funny about them? Compare your own reactions. This a great topic for small talk.

Next steps

Good storytellers often tell the same stories, but they tell them to different people. It is a good idea to prepare your own stories in advance. Good topics include:

- travelling, especially to strange or dangerous places.
- language misunderstandings.
- how you got your job.
- why you live where you live.
- your first job.

To prepare your story, follow these five steps.

1 Write your story. Try to use no more than 150 words. Stories shouldn't be long, but they have to be entertaining.
2 Record your story. How long did it take you to tell it? Can you make it shorter?
3 Listen to your recording. Does your story have a clear beginning, middle and end?
4 Improve the story.
5 Repeat steps 1–4 until you are satisfied. Then make sure you can tell your story without reading the text.

You could also tell a joke in English, but make sure the content is appropriate. Telling a joke in another language can be difficult, but it is rewarding when you hear your listeners laugh at the end.

> Do you know the funniest joke in the world? Richard Wiseman of the University of Hertfordshire believes he has found it. In 2002 he created a website where people could submit jokes and rate them. The winning joke came from Gurpal Gosal of Manchester, England. You can read it at:
> www.richardwiseman.com/LaughLab
>
> Try telling it to your colleagues. It usually gets a laugh.

 Go to www.collinselt.com/businessresources to listen to the real-life audio for this chapter.

Sensitive topics

My goals
- Make small talk without causing offence
- Discuss sensitive topics
- Deal with insensitive questions

Quiz

Ask yourself: 'Can I deal with difficult situations and avoid conflict?'

	Absolutely	Sometimes	No, I don't
I know which topics and what kind of body language could cause offence.	☐	☐	☐
I get angry when people seem critical of my culture, country or traditions.	☐	☐	☐
I know how to react to an insensitive question in a way that avoids conflict or embarrassment.	☐	☐	☐
I know how to discuss sensitive topics in a way that builds trust and respect.	☐	☐	☐
I can apologize if I inadvertently cause offence.	☐	☐	☐

Study focus

When you work internationally, you don't always know everything about your business partner's culture. So it is possible to make a mistake and end up offending someone. If this happens, you need to know how to deal with the situation. It may also be the case that someone offends you by asking a personal question, for example. You need to know how to respond.

Key phrases

Avoiding the topic or changing the subject

This is a little awkward/embarrassing, but we (don't/wouldn't) normally do/say that.

Actually/To be honest, I'd prefer not to talk about it.

To tell you the truth, I wouldn't know.

You know, I really couldn't say.

Showing understanding about a mistake

Never mind. / No problem. / Forget about it.

Don't worry about it. / No need to apologize.

It doesn't matter. / It's a common mistake.

I totally understand.

Clearing up misunderstandings or acknowledging a mistake

Sorry. Did I say/do something wrong?

(I'm) sorry. I had no idea. / (I'm) sorry. I didn't know.

Forgive me. I should have known that. / I completely forgot.

How insensitive/inconsiderate of me!

I'm so sorry. I really didn't mean to criticize/be rude.

I apologize. You must think I'm terribly insensitive.

I appreciate you telling me. / I appreciate that you told me.

Reacting sensitively to bad news

I'm so sorry (to hear that).

I hope he/she gets/feels better soon.

Please send/give him/her my best wishes.

How terrible! / That's awful!

My condolences/sympathies. / Please accept my condolences.

If there's anything I can do, let me know.

 Go to www.collinselt.com/businessresources
to listen to the key phrases.

Scenarios

Francine: How was the food on the flight?

Nasser: I didn't have any.

Francine: You must be hungry. Would you like some lunch?

Nasser: No, but thanks for asking. I'm fine.

Francine: We do have time for a quick bite, you know.

Nasser: **This is a little awkward, but** it's Ramadan right now and we don't eat until after sunset.

Francine: **Oh, I'm sorry. I completely forgot. You must think I'm terribly rude.**

Nasser: **No need to apologize.** But if you're hungry, please eat something.

Francine: No, no, it's OK. I'll eat later. **I appreciate you telling me.**

Markus: So, Petros, how's your wife?

Petros: Er, I thought you'd heard. She died a few months ago.

Markus: **Oh, I'm so sorry! Please accept my condolences.**

Petros: It was very sudden. I thought I'd told you.

Markus: No, **I had no idea. How terrible! If there's anything I can do** to make things easier for you, **please let me know.**

Petros: Thank you. **Actually, I'd prefer not to talk about it.**

Markus: **I totally understand.**

Petros: Anyway, let's look at that report together.

 Go to www.collinselt.com/businessresources to listen to the scenarios.

Over to you

1 What can you say if you have made a mistake? Complete the words in the sentences.

1 Did I say something **w** _ _ _ **g**?

2 You must think I'm terribly **r** _ _ **e**.

3 I didn't mean to be **ins** _ _ _ _ _ _ _ **e**.

4 How **inc** _ _ _ _ _ _ _ _ **te** of me!

2 What can you say if you don't want to talk about something? Put the words in the correct order. Don't forget to add punctuation.

1 tell / truth / you / to / the / know / wouldn't / I

....

2 prefer / to / be / I'd / it / not / honest / talk / to / about

....

3 couldn't / you / really / say / know / I

....

4 wouldn't / awkward / this / is / do / a / we / normally / little / that / but

....
....

3 What can you say to show someone that their mistake isn't a problem? Complete the useful phrases with the words in the box.

common	forget	matter	mind	need	worry

1 Never ....

2 Don't .... about it.

3 .... about it.

4 No .... to apologize.

5 It doesn't ....

6 It's a .... mistake.

4 **Complete the dialogues with the correct form of the missing verbs.**

1 Philippe: So, I see England did well in the rugby yesterday. You must be pleased.

  Angus: Not especially. I'm Scottish.

  Philippe: Oh, I'm sorry. I .... no idea.

2 Juan: Will John be joining us for lunch?

  Tom: Oh, didn't you hear? He's in hospital. He had an accident last week. I thought you knew.

  Juan: No, I'm so sorry. I hope he .... better soon. Please .... him my best wishes.

3 Hans: This is a little awkward, but we don't normally use first names here.

  Randy: You must .... I'm terribly rude. I ....

4 Carmen: I'm not very comfortable answering that question.

  Andrew: I'm sorry. I really didn't .... to be rude.

5 Bob: I was sorry to hear about your daughter.

  Rachel: To be honest, I'd rather not discuss this.

  Bob: I'm sorry. I totally ....

5 **How would you react?**

1 Someone asks you a personal question that you don't want to answer. You say:

....

2 You have to explain to someone that they have done something that may cause offence. You say:

....

3 Someone tells you that they don't want to answer a question you have asked. You say:

....

Tips: Dealing with difficult topics

If you find that your business partner is making comments that you strongly disagree with or dislike, you could:

- change the subject.

- ignore the comment(s) and talk about something else.

- say that you would rather not talk about the subject.

- make an excuse to leave – if possible. (See Chapter 13.)

As a rule, avoid talking about religion and politics. However, these topics may be hard to ignore if you are visiting a place after an election or other important event. And remember: *how* you talk about a topic can be more important than the topic itself. It is important not to appear critical of someone's culture. Don't make judgements based on your own culture, traditions or beliefs.

Direct personal questions are definitely taboo, whatever the topic. Here are some more tips.

- Don't ask direct personal questions about religion, but you can show a general interest in religious festivals.
  What do you do during Hanukkah/Diwali/Ramadan?

- Don't ask questions about people's incomes, but you can ask about the economy or the cost of living.
  Is it expensive to eat out here?

- Don't ask direct or negative questions about politics, but you can ask general questions.
  Will the recent election change anything?

- When asking questions about sensitive topics, you can ask more general questions that are open to interpretation.
  What are your thoughts on recent events?
  Would you mind explaining how it works here?

  You may have a business partner who is happy to discuss taboo or sensitive topics in great detail, but if they are not, they can choose to answer the question more briefly. If they give short answers, don't use follow-up questions. Instead, try a different topic.

Language focus: Contradicting politely

In Germany a direct contradiction or a direct 'no' doesn't usually cause offence. It is generally accepted that people will express themselves in this way. In most other cultures, however, particularly in Asia, people avoid contradicting each other directly. In such cultures it is important to try to keep a harmonious atmosphere. When working internationally, especially when making small talk, it is best to adopt an indirect style of communication.

If you must contradict someone, do so indirectly, and avoid saying 'no'.

Well, that's not entirely true, but I know what you mean.
Not really. / Not especially. / Not as far as I know.
Well, not exactly. / I wouldn't say so.
As a matter of fact, I don't think so.
Actually, it's not as bad as you might think.

Remember this! Taboo gestures

- What does it mean to you when someone makes a circle sign with their thumb and index finger?
  In many cultures it means 'OK'.
  In Japan it means 'money'.
  In France it means 'zero'.
  In Brazil it is a very rude gesture.

- What does it mean when you hold up five fingers with the palm facing outward?
  In many cultures it means 'five' or 'stop'.
  In Greece it is an extremely rude gesture.

As you can see, even the most simple hand gestures can be problematic and misunderstood, so find out what gestures are typically used in the countries where you do business. There are lots of books on intercultural communication and information on the internet.

The following include some useful information about cultural differences and taboos.

- *Key Business Skills* by Barry Tomalin
- *Essential Do's and Taboos: The Complete Guide to International Business and Leisure Travel* by Roger E Axtell

Next steps

Don't believe all the negative press about a place. Bad news sells. You can find out a more truthful version by reading about your business partners' countries in different sources. Learn about a country's history, politics, art and religion. Find out about regional differences too.

Use the **SMART** method (see Chapter 5) to improve your understanding of news stories about the countries you regularly visit or about your industry. This will help you to make small talk when you visit the country.

Specific: Read one short news story in English every week. Choose one relevant to you.

Measurable: Choose a few useful key words from a news item. Write the words on a piece of paper and stick them on your computer or on a wall next to your desk. Every time you have a break, look at the words and try to remember the details of the story you read. At the end of the week, write down as much as you can remember of the story and then check it against the original. How did you do?

Achievable: Choose stories that are short and not too difficult. At first, you could focus on just one paragraph.

Realistic: If you focus on news stories about your industry, read about them in your own language first. This will make it easier for you to understand the news in English.

Time: Decide how much time you want to spend on this activity and keep to that time.

A task while you travel

If you are staying in a hotel, sit in the lobby and watch how people interact. How do they greet each other? What do they say? Do they shake hands or kiss? What hand gestures do they use? You can also watch people at places like airports, train stations and conferences.

 Go to www.collinselt.com/businessresources to listen to the real-life audio for this chapter.

My goals

- End a conversation politely
- Make people want more
- Look to the future

Quiz

Ask yourself: 'Do I say goodbye in a way that makes people want to meet me again?'

	Absolutely	Sometimes	No, I don't
When I've met someone for the first time, I say goodbye in a polite and friendly way.	☐	☐	☐
At social events I move smoothly from one conversation partner to another.	☐	☐	☐
In difficult situations I know how to make a polite excuse to leave.	☐	☐	☐
I show that I have enjoyed meeting someone.	☐	☐	☐
I know what language and body language to use to bring a conversation to a close.	☐	☐	☐

Study focus

When it is time to say goodbye, you will need to use different key phrases and strategies, depending on the situation. If you have just met someone for the first time, you will say something different from what you will say to someone you meet every day at work or on a regular basis. In some situations you will be able to refer to a future meeting.

Key phrases

Bringing the conversation to a close

Anyway, I'd better be going (if I want to catch my flight).

Is that the time? I'm afraid I really should get going.

If you'll excuse me, I have to rush/I should make a move.

Saying goodbye

It was great/good/nice/a pleasure to meet you.

(You have my card, so) feel free to contact me any time.

Give me a call the next time you're in London.

I hope to see you at next year's conference. Are you going?

It's been really nice/great/fun talking to you again/in person.

Well, it was great/good/nice to see you again.

Getting out of a difficult conversation

Please excuse me (for a moment). I have to make a phone call.

Would you excuse me? I have to take care of something.

Looking to the future

So, we'll see each other next week.

Right then, we'll/I'll be in touch soon.

Keep in touch! / Keep me posted!

I look forward to seeing you (again).

Thanking the host and guest

Thank you for everything. It's been really great/useful.

Thanks (again) for your hospitality. / Thanks for coming.

Saying a final goodbye

(Have a) safe trip back/home.

Goodbye. / All the best. / Take care. / Bye (for) now. /
See you soon.

 Go to www.collinselt.com/businessresources
to listen to the key phrases.

Scenarios

Mateo: Well, it was great talking to you again.

Ranjini: Yes, it was. **And I hope to see you at the conference in Dubai. Are you going?**

Mateo: Yes, I am. It's an important market for us.

Ranjini: **I look forward to seeing you there. Take care!**

Mateo: You too! **Bye for now.**

Ranjini: **Bye.**

Mette: What do you think of my idea? Are you interested?

John: Oh! **Is that the time? Would you excuse me? I have to make a phone call.** I'm sorry.

Mette: Of course. No problem.

Paul: **Well, I'd better be going if I want to catch my flight.**

Sahid: Yes, of course. **I should make a move as well.** I have another meeting in 20 minutes.

Paul: So, it was a good trip. It was great to meet the team.

Sahid: Yes, **it was really nice to see you again. Thanks for coming.** My secretary will see you out. Your taxi should be waiting.

Paul: Fantastic. **Thanks again for your hospitality.**

Sahid: You're welcome. **Have a safe trip back. We'll be in touch soon.**

Paul: Great. **Bye.**

Sahid: **Bye.**

 Go to www.collinselt.com/businessresources to listen to the scenarios.

Over to you

1 Complete the sentences with the verbs in the box.

| be | feel | give | hope | look | see |

1 .... me a call the next time you're in Munich.

2 We'll .... each other next week.

3 .... free to contact me at any time.

4 I .... forward to it.

5 I .... to see you in Delhi.

6 I'll .... in touch next week.

2 What can you say to bring a conversation to a close? Complete the words in the sentences.

1 S _ , I'll see you next week.

2 R _ _ _ _ t _ _ _ , I'll call you tomorrow.

3 Is t _ _ _ the t _ _ _ ? I really should get going.

4 W _ _ _ , it was great to see you again.

5 Any _ _ _ , I'll see you at the next conference.

3 What can you say to get out of a difficult situation? Put the words in the correct order. Don't forget to add punctuation.

1 you / me / for / excuse / moment / would / a

....

2 I / me / you'll / excuse / have / phone / to / a / make / if / call

....

....

3 care / me / for / excuse / take / something / I / have / to / of /
a / moment

....

....

4 **What can you say to signal that you have to leave? Choose the correct word.**

1 I have to **rush / rushing**.

2 I really should get **go / going**.

3 I'd better **be / being** going.

4 I look forward to **see / seeing** you again.

5 Thanks for **come / coming**.

6 It's **been / being** really great to meet you in person.

5 **Match and make useful expressions.**

1	Thanks for	a	trip!
2	Keep me	b	everything.
3	Keep in	c	posted.
4	Take	d	best!
5	Safe	e	care!
6	All the	f	touch.
7	Thank	g	back.
8	Have a safe trip	h	you for your hospitality.

6 **What can you say to bring a conversation to a close? Complete the sentences with your own words.**

1 I'd better be going if I want to ....

2 If you'll excuse me, I have to ....

3 Is that the time? I'm afraid I ....

4 I have to rush. It's been ....

5 Thanks for coming. I hope to ....

Language focus: Closing a conversation

Native speakers of English often use idiomatic language when they say goodbye. Listen out for such language and how people respond. You may not feel confident enough to use these expressions, but you should expect to hear them and be able to react to them. For example, when people use the expression 'See you later', they often don't mean it literally.

Goodbye	Response
Shall we call it a day?	*Good idea. It's pretty late.*
Right then, I'm off.	*So soon?*
I'll catch you later.	*Great. See you then.*
I'll get back to you on Monday.	*Thanks. Don't forget.*
Say hello to Paula.	*Will do.*
Give my regards to Sam.	*I will.*
See you later.	*You too.*

Scenario

Brian: Well, I'd better be off.

Louise: Me too. I'll be in touch about the schedule.

Brian: Thanks. That would be great. Oh, and I'll get back to you on Monday about that software.

Louise: Oh, thanks. Do say hello to Paula, won't you?

Brian: Will do.

Louise: Right then. I'm off too.

Brian: Bye now. And thanks again. See you later.

Louise: You too. Keep me posted.

Before you leave, check that you have someone's contact details, especially if it was your first meeting.

Mike: Do you have a business card?

Vitesse: Sorry, didn't I give you one? Here you are.

Mike: You've got mine, I think.

Vitesse: I have. Thanks. I'll be in touch.

Remember this! Closing a conversation

Your body language can signal that you want to end a conversation. Here are some things you can do.

- Look at your watch. Then make a comment about the time.
- If you are sitting down, stand up. Don't stand up too quickly or too suddenly or you could appear rude.
- Offer a handshake. However, if you are in the Middle East or India, it may not be appropriate.

Pay attention to other people's body language too; it may show that they need to leave even if they haven't said so. Look out for these signs.

- They often look around the room or at their watch.
- They look in their bag or at their phone.
- They are silent.

Language focus: Future forms

When you talk about the future, you need to use various future forms.

- **Will** is the most useful and common future form for talking about the future. Use it to make a promise or an offer of help.
  I'll get back to you next week.
  I'll help you with those bags.
- Use **going to** to talk about plans and intentions.
  We're going to attend the conference in Delhi next month.
- Use the **present continuous** to talk about future arrangements that have already been finalized.
  We're flying to Canada in a week for our annual holiday.
- Use the **present simple** to talk about fixed schedules.
  My flight leaves at seven thirty tomorrow morning.
- Use the **future continuous** to ask a polite question about someone's plans.
  What time will you be leaving tomorrow?

Next steps

Once you have left a conference or a colleague's office and are travelling, what can you do to improve your English? What do you do while you are waiting at the gate to get on a plane? Or waiting in a line? Or for your meal or coffee to be served? This is 'dead' time and you can make the most of it to improve your English.

Here are some ideas for how you can make the most of the time on your own – and your 'dead' time. Test yourself or do mini-tasks to improve your English.

- If there is a free Wi-Fi connection and you have a mobile device, go online and read an article on a news site. Count the words you know in the top story on the homepage. Choose two words that you don't know and look them up in an online dictionary. You can access the *Collins COBUILD Advanced Dictionary* online at www.collinsdictionary.com/cobuild

- Look around you and try to describe the scene outside the window. What can you see? What is the weather like? What time of day is it? Think about the people you know at work and imagine what they might be doing right now. Try and describe the scene.

- Spend ten minutes reviewing some vocabulary. Carry your language cards or notebook with you. Or use a language app on your phone.

- Look at the person opposite you – but don't stare! Imagine what kind of work they do and what kind of person they are. Invent a career for them using your imagination – in English, of course. If you can't think of a word, look it up.

 Go to www.collinselt.com/businessresources to listen to the real-life audio for this chapter.

My goals
- Make small talk on the phone or via video conference
- Contribute in group virtual meetings
- Explain and deal with technical problems

Quiz

Ask yourself: 'Can I connect with people on the phone and in virtual meetings?'

	Absolutely	Sometimes	No, I don't
To get phone calls off to a good start, I spend a few minutes on small talk.	☐	☐	☐
I make small talk in conference calls even if there are a lot of people.	☐	☐	☐
I know how to explain that I'm having technical problems.	☐	☐	☐
I enjoy video conferences and feel that I contribute to them.	☐	☐	☐
I know how to end a phone call or a conference call.	☐	☐	☐

Study focus

Small talk at a distance is just as important as during face-to-face meetings. However, communicating when you can't see your business partner's body language can be more difficult than communicating face to face. This chapter focuses on strategies for talking to people at a distance, either on the phone (when there are two people), via a conference call (when there are three or more people) or via a video conference or an online meeting such as Skype™ or Google Hangouts.

Key phrases

Opening

Hi, it's Joe. / Hi, this is Joe (speaking). / Hi, Joe here.

How are you this morning/today, Pete?

Are you busy? Is this a good time to talk?

Kick-starting a meeting

How are things at the head office/over there?

What's the weather like at your end/over there?

What's the time difference (again)?

We're three hours behind/ahead.

You should really try to make the next meeting in person.

Ending a call

It's been great talking to you. I'll be in touch.

I'll let you get back to your work. / I don't want to keep you.

I'm running a little late. I'll let you go.

Have a nice evening/weekend!

Getting out of a call

I'm a little busy at the moment/right now.

Actually, you've caught me at a bad time. Can I call you back in an hour?

To be honest, I was about to leave. It's the end of our day here.

Group meetings

OK, is everyone here?

Can we all say our names so we know who's here?

We're all here. This is Philippe. I'm here with John and Julie.

John's running a little late. / John's just walked in.

Let's get started. Does everyone have the agenda?

That's it for today. Thank you everyone. / Thanks for your time.

 Go to www.collinselt.com/businessresources
to listen to the key phrases.

Scenarios

June:	Hi Sue. **Is this a good time to talk? It's June.**
Sue:	June, hi. I saw it was your number. **Actually, you've caught me at a bad time. I was just about to leave. It's 8 p.m. here.**
June:	Oh, I'm sorry, I got the time difference wrong. We've just had lunch. I thought it was only 5 p.m.
Sue:	**We're three hours ahead.**
June:	I'm sorry. I'll call you tomorrow. It's not urgent.
Sue:	Thanks, June. **I'll let you get back to work.**
June:	**Have a nice evening!**

Hasim:	**OK, can we all say our names so we know who's here?**
Li:	**This is Li. I'm here with Sue and Randolph.** Hi everyone!
Sahid:	**Sahid here.** Good morning.
Hasim:	OK, **John's running a little late.** So, Li, **what's the weather like at your end?**
Li:	Good. Quite sunny. **How are things over there?**
Hasim:	Not too bad. We've all just had lunch together. **You should really try to make the next meeting in person.** Oh! **John's just walked in.**
Li:	**Li here.** Hi John.
John:	Hi everyone.
Sahid:	**This is Sahid.** Good morning, John.
Hasim:	OK, **let's get started.**

 Go to www.collinselt.com/businessresources
to listen to the scenarios.

Over to you

1 What can you say during group phone calls and video conferences? Put the words in the correct order. Don't forget to add punctuation.

1 who's / here / names / can / know / all / say / our / we / so / we

....

2 everyone / have / let's / get / agenda / does / the / started

....

3 for / that's / everyone / it / thank / today / you

....

4 really / meeting / you / person / should / try / to / the / in / next / make

....

5 OK / everyone / hear / can

....

6 just / we've / lunch / had / together / all

....

2 Which sentence in exercise 1 would you use to ...

a check the sound quality? ....

b check who's there? ....

c make small talk? ....

d change the subject to a business focus? ....

e suggest that someone should come to the next meeting? ....

f end the call? ....

3 What can you say at the start of a phone call? Match the sentence beginnings with the sentence endings.

1 Is this a good   a like at your end?

2 How are   b busy?

3 What's the weather   c you this morning?

4 Are you   d time to talk?

4 **Re-arrange the letters in brackets and complete the sentences.**

1 We're three hours ...., so I've just arrived. (hibend)

2 What's the time .... again? (dicefenref)

3 We're four hours ...., so I'm leaving. (daaeh)

4 How are you this .... ? (rimnong)

5 I'm a little busy .... now. (girth)

5 **What can you say to end a conversation? Complete the sentences with the correct form of the verbs in the box.**

catch	get	keep	leave	let	run	talk	want

1 I'll .... you .... back to your work.

2 I don't .... to .... you.

3 Actually, I'm .... a little late.

4 It's been great .... to you.

5 Actually, you've .... me at a bad time.

6 To be honest, I was just about to ....

6 **Complete the dialogue.**

Nathan: Good morning. Is this a good time to talk?

You: **(1)** *(Explain that it is not a good time.)*

....

Nathan: Oh, I'm sorry. I got the time difference wrong.

You: **(2)** *(Explain the time difference and say what the time is.)*

....

Nathan: I'm sorry. I'll call you on Monday. It can wait.

You: **(3)** *(Say thank you and end the conversation with a positive comment.)*

....

Nathan: Have a nice evening.

Tips: Video conferences and online meetings

Video conferences and online meetings often involve groups of people from all over the world, so they are often scheduled at precise times. Generally, meetings follow a tight agenda, especially when participants join from different time zones. As a result of this and the fact that there are lots of people in the meeting, small talk is usually kept to a minimum.

Do's

- Look at the webcam or camera, not at your keyboard or out of the window.

- Make sure your webcam is at the right angle so that you look your best. If you are in a video conference, make sure you are close enough to the camera to be seen.

- Make sure your work space is tidy if you are making the call from your office. It makes a good impression.

- Turn off your webcam if the connection is slow or if the image freezes. It is better to have a clear sound than an image that keeps breaking up.

- If you are having a meeting with colleagues that you know well, try to direct the small talk to areas they are interested in. But if you are part of a bigger group, don't direct your questions or comments to one person only.

- If you are waiting for someone to join the meeting, make comments about what you can see, for example: 'So, the sun is shining over there, I see.'

Don't's

- Don't multitask during a call. Even if the webcam is off, people will hear you typing or will hear any other sounds that your computer makes, for example a 'ping' when you send an email.

- Don't eat or drink during the call. The sounds you make might be audible.

- Don't move papers around. The sound can be distracting.

Language focus: Describing technical problems

Technology is not always reliable, so it is important to be able to describe any technical problems you may be having. Here are some useful key phrases for checking that everyone is happy with the quality of the meeting and for describing any problems.

- **Checking that everyone can hear/see you**

  Can everyone see/hear me OK?

- **Explaining the problem**

  I can't see you, Paul. Can you check that your webcam is on?
  The video keeps freezing. / The picture has frozen again.
  I can't see the presentation/document online.
  The sound isn't good. You keep breaking up.
  There seems to be some static on the line.
  We can't hear you. Can you check your microphone?
  I can't hear you. Can you hear me?
  Sorry, we're having some technical problems.
  Sorry about that. I lost my internet connection for a moment.

- **Suggesting a solution**

  Could you all turn off your mobile phones?
  Should I turn off the webcam and see if that improves the sound quality?
  Shall we hang up and try again?

- **Confirming that everything is OK**

  Everything is working perfectly. / The picture is great now.
  The sound is much better now, thanks.
  I'm back again.

- **Taking control of the conversation**

  Could you slow down/speak up a little, please?
  Could I just interrupt you for a moment?
  Can you say that last bit again, please?

- **Checking who is speaking**

  Sorry, is that Markus?
  Could you say your name before you speak?

Next steps

Working with your phone

You don't need an expensive smartphone to make the most of mobile learning opportunities. Find out if your mobile phone will allow you to do the following.

- Record yourself while you make a phone call. Use your mobile phone to record you while you talk on your landline.

- Record other people (but first ask if you can). You could put them on the speakerphone on your landline and record them on your mobile phone. Play back the recording and focus on the language they used. Could you use it too?

- Record yourself using the key phrases when you have a free moment. Listen to your pronunciation and intonation. Do you speak clearly? Do you sound interested?

Virtual events

- Sign up for a free online conference on a topic that interests you or watch a presenter on YouTube.

- Watch the body language of the host and moderators.

- Pay attention to the language that the presenter uses to make sure everyone can hear and understand what is happening.

- Is there a chatroom area? Is there any small talk going on in there? Make a note of the topics people are talking about. Join in!

Being prepared

Write the key phrases that you think you will need on small pieces of paper and place them by your phone. Imagine you are on the phone using the phrases. How do you think the person you are calling will respond to them? Imagine different scenarios and practise them in your head before you pick up the phone to make a call. The more you practise, the easier it will be to use the key phrases when you need them.

 Go to www.collinselt.com/businessresources to listen to the real-life audio for this chapter.

15 Email exchanges

My goals
- Begin and end an email with small talk
- Maintain good relationships through email
- Switch to business after small talk

Quiz

Ask yourself: 'Do I use email as an opportunity for building relationships?'

	Absolutely	Sometimes	No, I don't
I prefer to write formal emails to business partners.	☐	☐	☐
I write something friendly at the beginning of an email.	☐	☐	☐
Emails are a fast way to communicate, so I write them quickly and not very carefully.	☐	☐	☐
When I use an informal style of writing, I think my emails look unprofessional.	☐	☐	☐
I end my emails with a personal message.	☐	☐	☐

Study focus

Writing clear professional emails is an essential business skill. As a rule, small talk often begins and ends an email: it wraps around the business content of the message. This chapter focuses on writing emails to people you regularly communicate with.

Key phrases

Making a friendly start
Hi John / Morning John / John
I hope you're well. / I hope you're enjoying the spring weather.
How are you? / How's it going?

Following up after a visit or other contact
Thank you for your kind hospitality.
It was good/great to see you again.

Showing interest/Sharing information
Welcome back!
(I) hope you had a good break/weekend/conference.
(I) hope you're feeling better.
How are things at headquarters/in Tokyo?
(I) hope you're not working too hard/you're not too busy!
(I) hope you're enjoying the sunshine/weather/football.
I've just got back from Finland and it was fabulous.
The weather is perfect/amazing/awful here today.

Ending the email
Have a nice/lovely/relaxing/fun weekend.
See you soon/on Monday.
Looking forward to seeing/meeting you.
Have a good break/flight/weekend.
(I) hope you enjoy your stay/trip/break.

Signing off
Greetings from sunny Dubai/rainy Manchester.
Very best wishes / Bye for now / Take care!
All the best / Best
Thanks! / Thanks again for everything.
Best/Kind regards

Scenarios

Subject   Arrangements for your trip and new designs

Hi John

How are you? I hope you've had a good week. Have you packed your bags yet?

I just wanted to confirm that our driver will pick you up at the airport, at the usual place. We've also made a reservation at your favourite restaurant.

By the way, the new designs have already arrived. Please find them attached. We can look at them and discuss the layout in detail when you are in the office.

Looking forward to seeing you again. Have a good flight.

All the best
Lim

Subject   Thank you again

Hi Lim

Thank you so much for your kind hospitality. It was great to see you again — and to eat chilli crab. I wish I could find a restaurant that serves it a bit closer to my home!

Anyway, I'm pleased that we were able to choose a final design. The trip was very productive. I'm looking forward to seeing the prototype.

Thanks again for everything.

Best
John

Over to you

1 What can you say to begin an email? Complete the phrases with your own words.

1 Hope you're not ....

2 I hope you're ....

3 How .... ?

4 How's .... ?

2 What can you say to end an email? Complete the phrases with your own words.

1 Looking forward to ....

2 Have a ....

3 Bye for ....

4 All the ....

5 Take ....

6 Thanks again ....

3 Complete this sentence in as many ways as you can:
It was great to ...

....

....

....

....

....

....

4 Tick the expressions that might be too informal for an email to someone you don't know very well or who has a higher position in the company than you.

1 How's it going? ....

2 Hope you're not working too hard. ....

3 I hope you are enjoying the sunshine. ....

4 I hope you are well. ....

5 Warm greetings from rainy London. ....

6 Kind regards ....

7 Best ....

5 What can you say to someone after returning from a visit to their office? Complete the email with your own words.

1 Write three sentences about your trip.

2 Write a closing statement.

3 Sign off and write your name.

Subject	_____

Hi Raffi

(1) Thank you _____

_____

_____

Anyway, I'm pleased that we were able to discuss the schedule in more detail. It was good to meet the whole team and I'm sure we will work well together.

(2) _____

(3) _____

_____

Tips: Writing professional emails

- **Small talk:** Don't overdo the small talk in business emails. It can be distracting.

- **Subjects for small talk:** Use key phrases from other chapters in this book in your emails so that you can include a variety of topics.

- **Subject line:** Never forget to add a subject line, even in an informal email.

- **Start and/or finish:** Add a short small talk comment to the beginning of an email and/or to the end.

- **Style:** You can use informal language when you write to people quite often, but people with a higher position than you in the company or clients usually expect a more formal tone. If you are writing the first email ever to someone, it is generally best to begin with 'Dear Mr/Mrs/Ms ...' and end with 'Kind/Best regards'.

- **Smileys:** Emoticons show how you feel about something you have written in an email. By adding a smiley :-) to the end of a comment, you can indicate that you are saying something with a smile and hope that the reader will find your comment funny or not take it too seriously. However, it is not a good idea to use emoticons in business emails; many business people don't like them.

- **Signatures:** Formal emails usually end with a signature that includes your position, company address and email address. Informal emails often have a shorter signature or none at all. It is a good idea to set up different signatures depending on the kind of email you are writing – and to include your phone number. This saves people time if they want to call you about something in your email.

- **Spelling:** Even in informal emails, make use of the spellcheck. You want to be informal, not unprofessional.

- **Short forms:** You can use abbreviations in informal emails, but don't use too many in the same email. Here are some common abbreviations.
  BTW = by the way
  ASAP = as soon as possible
  FYI = for your information

Language focus: Changing the subject

If you start your email with small talk, you will probably need to change the subject to focus on business. Here are some common informal phrases you could use.

BTW (= by the way), *I can confirm that Mark will be taking over as team leader.*

By the way, *I spoke to Madeleine about the files and she ...*

Anyway, back to work!

Anyway, *I was talking to John about the software and ...*

(I) just wanted to let you know *that Madeleine will be coming to the presentation.*

I was wondering if *you've made a final decision.*

So, *I've read your comments on the changes to the system ...*

One more thing, *I'll be attending the conference in June ...*

Some expressions are also be used to change the subject from a business focus to small talk.

BTW, *I hope you enjoyed the football last night. I saw that your team won. You must celebrate!*

Anyway, *I'll be leaving the office soon. I have tickets for the theatre tonight and I don't want to be late.*

Hi Dima,

Welcome back! I hope you had a productive trip. How was the weather in Moscow? It's awful here in Oslo!

Anyway, back to work. I just wanted to let you know that I've spoken to Markus about the changes to the software and he agrees that they are necessary. Can you send me a detailed list of the problems by 10:00 tomorrow morning? I have a meeting with Markus at 15:00 and would like to discuss the problems with him then.

BTW, I won't be in the office next week as I'm visiting my family in Rome. I'm looking forward to some sunny weather again.

Bye for now
Angela

Next steps

You can learn useful expressions and phrases from the emails that your business partners send you.

- Check the emails in your inbox for small talk. Do some of your colleagues or business partners use small talk regularly? Do some people not include small talk at all? What kind of business relationship do you have with the people who make small talk with you? Is it more friendly and relaxed?

- Check the kind of small talk that people use. Is there a difference in the kind of small talk people make when they email you more frequently?

- Check your emails to see if people have a favourite topic. Is your business partner a football fan or into fitness? Share different information depending on people's interests. However, try not to repeat the same phrases or information when you write to them each time. Change the focus and the language to show that you are genuinely interested.

- Check your emails to see how much personal information people want to share with you. It is best not to ask too many questions.

- Finally, create a file on your computer. Copy and paste key phrases from emails that make a positive impression on you. Refer to the file before you write an email. Over time, you will learn these phrases and will be able to use them as required.

My goals
- Invite someone to connect
- Post messages and comments
- Share articles and updates

Quiz

Ask yourself: 'Do I know how to use social media to boost relationships and raise my profile?'

	Absolutely	Sometimes	No, I don't
When I make new contacts, I look them up on professional networking sites.	☐	☐	☐
I think it's unprofessional to contact business partners on social media.	☐	☐	☐
I know how to invite someone to connect.	☐	☐	☐
I feel confident about posting messages.	☐	☐	☐
I use social media to share articles with business partners and colleagues.	☐	☐	☐

Study focus

Many business people use professional networking sites such as LinkedIn®, InterNations, XING, Facebook or Twitter to build their networks. Your company may have created its own corporate online network, for example through Yammer. This chapter focuses on the language you need to communicate effectively on networking sites, whether your message is public (sharing an article) or more private (connecting with someone).

Key phrases

Inviting someone you know to connect

You may not remember me, but we spoke briefly at the BON conference in Dubai last month.

I saw you were on LinkedIn® and thought it would be good to connect/get in touch.

You may remember that we worked at the same company in 2010. Would you like to connect/keep in touch via Xing?

Responding to an invitation

Thanks very much for the invite/invitation.

Thanks for getting in touch. I'd be happy to connect with you.

Of course I remember talking to you.

I'm sorry, but can you remind me how we know each other?

I use Facebook just with close friends and family. Let's connect on LinkedIn® instead.

Sharing articles/updates

I thought this article might interest you.

Have you seen this website?

I thought of you when I read this. / Is this of any use to you?

Posting positive comments and thanks

Great article. Thanks for sharing.

I really enjoyed reading the article. Thanks.

That's good to know.

Commenting on birthdays, celebrations and good news

Congratulations on your new job/promotion!

(That's) awesome/wonderful/excellent news!

All the best (for your new job/the move)!

Well done! I'm sure you'll be a success.

I wish you every success.

Scenarios

Selina
Invitation to connect

Hi Selina

You may not remember me, but we spoke briefly at the tech conference in Toronto last week. We sat next to each other in the plenary. **I saw you were on LinkedIn and thought it would be good to get in touch.**

Kind regards
Deborah

Send   Cancel

Deborah
Re: Invitation to connect

Hi Deborah

Thanks very much for the invitation. I'd be happy to connect with you.

Are you going to the tech conference in Vancouver, by any chance? I hope to see you there.

All the best
Selina

Send   Cancel

Selina
Re: Invitation to connect

Hi Selina

Yes, I'll be at the conference. I'm staying at the conference hotel.

BTW, **have you seen this article** about the project I mentioned in Toronto? www. …
I thought it might interest you. As you can see, we're going ahead with the project and there may be an opportunity for you to work on our team. It would be good to meet up in Vancouver to discuss some options.

Let me know what you think. It would be good to see you there.
Deborah

Send   Cancel

Over to you

1 **Choose the correct word.**

1 You may not **remember / remind** me, but we met last week at the conference.

2 I'm sorry, but can you **remember / remind** me how we know each other?

3 Of course I **remember / remind** you.

4 You may **remember / remind** that we worked at the same company in 2010.

5 I **remember / remind** talking to you briefly in the break.

2 **What can you say to respond to an invitation? Complete the sentences with the words in the box.**

close	connect	instead	invitation	touch

1 Thanks very much for the .... !

2 Thanks for getting in ....

3 I'd be happy to .... with you.

4 I use Facebook just with .... friends and family. Let's connect on XING ....

3 **Match and make useful expressions.**

1	That's wonderful	**a**	news.
2	I wish you	**b**	done!
3	Congratulations	**c**	wishes.
4	All the best for	**d**	the move.
5	That's	**e**	on your promotion!
6	Well	**f**	you'll be a success.
7	I'm sure	**g**	every success.
8	Best	**h**	awesome!

4 **What can you say to recommend an article to someone? Put the words in the correct order. Don't forget to add punctuation.**

1 you / this / thought / I / interest / might

   ....

2 seen / have / article / you / this

   ....

3 I / this / you / I / thought / of / read / when

   ....

4 any / is / you / of / use / this / to

   ....

5 **What can you say to respond to a recommendation? Complete the words in the sentences.**

1 Thanks for **s** _ _ _ _ _ _ this article.

2 I really enjoyed **r** _ _ _ _ _ _ the article. Thanks.

3 That's good to **k** _ _ _ .

6 **Write your own invitation using the words in the box. Then think about the people you would like to add to your network. What could you add to personalize an invitation to them?**

may	remember	but	spoke	briefly	saw	on
thought	would	good	touch	like	connect	

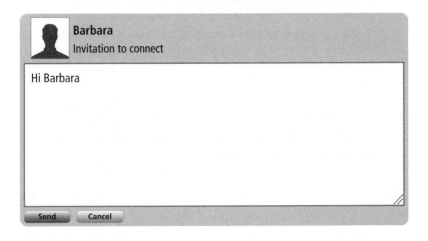

Barbara
Invitation to connect

Hi Barbara

Send   Cancel

Tips: Networking and raising your profile

Corporate networking sites

If your company has its own networking site, find out what people are using it for. You may be able to connect with people who can help you – or whom you can help.

Professional networking sites

- When you hand out your business card, let people know that you use networking sites and social media.
  Here's my card. You'll also find me on LinkedIn®.

- After a conference, seminar or event, invite any new contacts to connect. You may have each other's details now, but they could change in the future.

- Most sites have an automatic connection request, for example, 'I'd like to add you to my professional network', but it is better to write a personal message.

- In your invitations remind people how they know you.
  It was good to talk at the conference yesterday. Would you like to connect?

- Search for people you already know and add them to your network. You may learn something about them that can help you to understand them better and to create a better working relationship.

- Post updates that people will enjoy reading. Recommend interesting articles or reports. Some sites also allow you to start or join discussions and groups. If your posts are interesting, they may receive lots of comments, likes, retweets or recommendations and more people will see them.

- Don't post too many updates or share too many articles or it might look like you don't do any other work. Also, your business partners may not be pleased to receive constant updates and shared articles.

Remember this! Using Facebook and Twitter

Facebook

For many people, Facebook is for family and friends only. In some industries, however, it is also a great site for connecting with business partners. But be very careful how you combine work with pleasure.

- Use filters to limit who can see your photos and updates.
- Consider how your posts may affect the image of yourself that you present to colleagues.
- Set your profile so that you have to authorize or allow people to post on your timeline, comment on your posts and tag you in photos or posts.
- If you play games, check to see if your game updates are being posted automatically online. Do you want your colleagues and business partners to see them?

Twitter

Twitter is ideal for connecting with people before, during and after a conference or event. You may have to find them on another site first; people often have different user names on Twitter, so it can be difficult to find them.

Hashtags (#) are essential on Twitter. You use them to categorize your posts or to find posts that you are interested in. Check if there is a special hashtag for events and conferences and follow people who are using the hashtag in their tweets (messages). You can also send them a message and invite them to meet up at the conference.

Be aware that anything you post on general social media sites may be copied and reposted, even when you have your settings on the highest privacy level. You can never be sure that what you post will remain private, and once you do post something, it could remain online forever.

Next steps

It is a good idea to check out professional networking sites.

If you haven't already got a profile on a professional networking site such as **LinkedIn**®, experiment with one. If you have an account, think about what you could do to improve it.

- Your profile is your business card. Make sure it looks professional.
- Use a good, clear, professional photo.
- Keep your profile up to date, especially the section about your work.
- Request recommendations from colleagues and business partners.
- Join groups that focus on your interests and take an active part in them. But don't spam.

Use **Twitter** to learn English. Follow people you are interested in. Look at the topics that are 'trending' and read a few tweets. Set a time limit or you could spend hours on Twitter and it could take over your day.

Use **Facebook** to learn English. 'Like' the pages of English-language websites and start your day by looking at their feeds.

Depending on where you do business, you may like to check out other international networks.

- **ApnaCircle** is popular in India.
- **InterNations** is a global networking site, popular with expatriates.
- **Pinterest** is used for sharing information using Pins, which are visual bookmarks. It is popular in the US.
- **VIADEO** is popular in France.
- **XING** is used a lot in Germany, Austria and Switzerland.

Communication strategies

Top ten tips

1 **Use names.** Show that you are interested in someone by using their name when you begin and/or end a conversation.
So, Hasim, how was your flight?

2 **Let people talk.** You need to learn something about your business partner, so don't talk too much yourself.
So, tell me more about your trip to Thailand.

3 **Be encouraging.** Show that you are interested in what someone is saying by using 'noises', phrases or single words.
Uh-huh. / Oh. / Wow! / I see. / I understand. / Really?

4 **Ask open questions.** Use questions words like 'What' or 'Where'; they invite longer answers.
What did you think of the presentation?

5 **Be an echo.** Listen out for key words and repeat them to show that you want to hear more about a topic.
*A: I was in **Tokyo** last weekend.*
*B: **Tokyo**? It's a beautiful city. Do you go there often?*

6 **Share information about yourself.** This makes it easier for people to find a common interest with you.
I grew up in Spain, but live in Dublin now.

7 **Connect.** Find a connection to the things that people tell you. Even if you haven't shared an experience, try and find another way to connect.
*A: I was at a similar conference in **Shanghai** last week.*
*B: **Shanghai**? I've never been to China, but I'd love to go. How was the conference there?*

8 **Be positive and make compliments.** If you make people feel good about themselves, they will feel good about talking to you.
You look well. Have you been on holiday?

9 **Take turns.** Don't do all the talking and don't do all the listening.
What about you? What do you think of the conference?

10 **Always end small talk on a positive note.** It leaves people feeling good about you and the time they spent with you.
Well, it's been great talking to you, Hasim. I hope you have a good flight back.

Body language basics

Your body language should show that you are paying attention to your business partner and that you are interested in them.

- Look at people, smile and nod.
- Relax. Don't fold your arms in front of you; people may interpret this as a sign that you don't want to open up.
- Is your business partner mirroring your moves? If they are, it is a sign that they feel comfortable with you. Are you mirroring your business partner?

Spelling

When you meet people for the first time, they may not hear your name or your company name properly. And you may not hear theirs. It is important to be able to spell these details in a way that is easily understood. Here are some easy words that most people know and that you can use to spell out your details.

A for apple	H for happy	O for oranges	V for victory
B for book	I for iPhone	P for people	W for water
C for cat	J for jaguar	Q for queen	X for X-ray
D for dog	K for king	R for report	Y for yoga
E for easy	L for like	S for sugar	Z for zebra
F for face	M for money	T for tomato	
G for go	N for nobody	U for umbrella	

You will also need these symbols to say your email or email addresses.

- hyphen/dash	/ forward slash	. dot
_ underscore	@ at	

Numbers

How do you say your telephone number? Often, we split long numbers into groups of two or three digits. We say the international code first, then the local code, and then the number. For example, 44 20 ... is the number you give someone if they are ringing you in London from abroad. We can say 'double four, two zero ...'.

Answer key

1 New contacts

1   **1** c   **2** e   **3** a   **4** d   **5** b

2

1 **Ria:** Hello. I don't think we've been introduced. My name's Ria.

2 **John:** Oh, I'm so sorry, Ria! Sayuri, this is Ria Fisher, our company blogger in London. We work in the same building.

3 **Sayuri:** Nice to meet you, Ria.

4 **John:** Ria, this is Sayuri Riisa. She's one of our engineers here in Berlin.

5 **Ria:** It's great to meet you too, Sayuri.

6 **Sayuri:** Actually, I'm a fan of your blog, Ria.

7 **Ria:** Really? Thank you. It's nice of you to say that.

3

1 in Berlin

2 Ria and John

3 Ria

4 Sayuri

5 yes

6 Sayuri has read Ria's blog, but they have never met face to face before.

4

1 have/'ve met

2 saying

3 introduce

4 give

5 didn't catch

6 spell

5 **Model answers**

1 Hi. I don't think we've been introduced. I'm (your name).

2 It's good to meet you too. I'm sorry, but I didn't catch your last name.

3 It's (spell your name). Let me give you my business card.

6 See Part C: Communication strategies.

2 Old contacts

1 1 Long time no see!   3 How have you been?
      2 Good to see you again.   4 It's so good to finally meet you.

2 1 right   2 things   3 been   4 about

3 1 I'm sorry. How **could** I forget!
      2 I thought you were someone **else**.
      3 I can't **believe** we haven't met before!
      4 I'm sorry, but can you **jog/refresh** my memory?

4 **Model answer**
Paula: It's Jonathan, right?
John: Close. Actually, it's John. I don't think we've met.
Paula: I'm Paula Reed. We met at the conference in Hong Kong.
John: We did? I'm sorry, but you'll have to jog my memory.
Paula: We sat next to each other at the dinner.
John: Of course. I remember now. How could I forget!
Paula: It's good to see you again.
John: It's good to see you too. How are things, Paula?

5 **Model answers**
      1 Actually, it's/I'm (your name).
        No problem.
      2 That's right.
        I'm really sorry, but what's your name again?
        It's great to meet you, Ioannis.

3 Start networking

1   **1** d   **2** c   **3** a   **4** b

2   **Model answers**
1   Of course. Please take/have a seat.
2   Yes, it is. The venue is amazing, isn't it?
3   No, it's free. Please join us.
4   Not at all. Please do.

3   **1** c   **2** a   **3** d   **4** b

4   **1** venue   **2** atmosphere   **3** keynote   **4** thought

5   **1** impressive   **3** interesting   **5** outstanding
       2 valid   **4** terrible

6   **1** I know what you mean.
       2 I know the feeling.
       3 I know exactly how you feel.
       4 That's so true.

7   **Model answers**
1   Of course. Have a seat.
2   I know exactly how you feel. The last presentation was impressive, wasn't it?
3   Me too. And the venue is fantastic, isn't it?

4 Introducing the business

1
1	Past	3	Present	5	Present
2	Past	4	Present	6	Past

2 The questions in this exercise are about you. You should answer them using the key phrases in Chapter 4.

3
1	of	3	in	5	to / with
2	for	4	into		

4
1 What do you hope to get out of this event?
2 So, what brings you to this conference?
3 What line of business are you in?
4 How long have you been working there?

5
1	So	3	Really	5	That must be
2	Well	4	exactly	6	What about

6 The questions in this exercise are about you. You should answer them using the key phrases in Chapter 4.

---

5 On to business

1
1 Pharmaceuticals.
2 Igor's company uses an Irish company to package its drugs. Pierre's company is based in Ireland and offers the same service.
3 Pierre's company offers a similar service, so they might be able to do business together.

2
1	would	3	Sounds	5	work
2	like	4	be		

3
1. Actually
2. Speaking of
3. You know
4. By the way
5. That reminds me
6. Funny you should say that

4
1. Maybe we could get together and discuss this in detail.
2. Look, here's my card. Why don't you give me a call?
3. Well, I have your card, so I'll be in touch.

5
The questions in this exercise are about you. You should answer them using the key phrases in Chapter 5.

6 Great guests, perfect hosts

1
1. take
2. get
3. offer
4. pick
5. help

2
1. thirsty
2. tired
3. jet-lagged
4. hungry

3
1. **Nina:** Welcome to Kiev. How was your flight?
2. **Jules:** Very long. I'm glad to be back on the ground.
3. **Nina:** You must be tired.
4. **Jules:** No, I'm fine. I slept the whole trip. Thank you for picking me up, by the way.
5. **Nina:** My pleasure. It's very cold outside. Are you ready?
6. **Jules:** Yes, I am. I bought a new coat for this trip!
7. **Nina:** You'll need it. How was the weather in Sydney when you left?
8. **Jules:** Beautiful. Very sunny!
9. **Nina:** Well, don't expect to see much sun here during your trip.
10. **Jules:** I won't. So, how far is it to your office?

4
1. pleasure
2. problem
3. to see you (again)
4. to hear that

5
1. Let me help you with your luggage. / Can I help you with your luggage?
2. Please help yourself/yourselves to the sandwiches.
3. If there's anything you need, please just ask.
4. Can I offer you something to drink?

6 **Model answers**
1. It's great to see you too!
2. The flight was fine, thanks. How's the weather here?
3. No problem. I brought my new pair of sunglasses with me.

7 Opening up

1
1	old	3	many
2	did	4	everyone

2
1. Were/Weren't you born in Paris?
2. Are/Aren't you originally from Chennai?
3. How did you end up in Berlin?
4. Did/Didn't you grow up in France?
5. Have you always lived here?

3

Marital status	Partners	Special occasions	Relatives
single	husband	honeymoon	father-in-law
divorced	fiancé	anniversary	cousin
engaged	spouse	birthday	daughter
married	wife	wedding	grandchild
			mother-in-law
			step-child
			uncle

4
1 Is it two or three girls that you have?

2 Isn't your daughter studying in Berlin?

3 Haven't you just moved?

4 Don't you have a big dog?

5 Am I right in thinking you grew up in Malta?

5
1 remember   3 memory

2 asking   4 kind

6 This exercise is about you. You should answer it using the key phrases in Chapter 7.

---

8 Using everyday moments

1
1 **Mette:** How was your weekend, Beth?

2 **Beth:** Great, thanks. I finally got to see that movie with Tom Hanks that everyone's been talking about.

3 **Mette:** You did? What did you think of it?

4 **Beth:** Oh, it was long – but good. I like Tom Hanks.

5 **Mette:** Me too. I love his rom-coms, but my husband hates them.

6 **Beth:** Mine too, but he chose the last movie we went to.

7 **Mette:** Now that's a good system. I'll have to suggest it to my husband.

2
1 Do you get much time to play golf?

2 How was your vacation?

3 Have you got any plans for the festive season?

4 Have you read any interesting books lately?

5 How often do you go swimming?

3
1 Oh, nice. Going anywhere special?
   Oh, nice. Any plans?

2 You did? Any good?
   You did? I did too. / So did I. / Me too.

4

1	too	**3**	well	**5**	to
2	neither	**4**	more		

5   The questions in this exercise are about you. You should answer them using the key phrases in Chapter 8.

---

9 Who's who and what's what

1

1   Let me introduce you to the team.
2   Let me give you a tour of our offices.
3   Come and meet Andy.
4   Have you met everyone else?
5   I'd like to introduce you to the CEO.
6   Let me explain how our organization works.

2

1	up	**3**	for	**5**	of
2	in	**4**	with	**6**	for

3

1	conference	**3**	building	**5**	floor
2	location	**4**	open-plan	**6**	canteen

4

1	spectacular	**4**	interesting	**6**	good
2	lucky	**5**	convenient	**7**	around
3	cool				

5

1	Who	**4**	Could	
2	How	**5**	How many	
3	Where			

6 **Model answers**

1 My pleasure. Our open-plan offices are in a great location.

2 No. However, you will have the chance to meet John, our Sales Manager, Emma, our Finance Manager, and Sam, our Production Manager there. They all work for the European division.

3 Alex is in charge of Marketing in France and works closely with John, Emma and Sam.

10 Entertaining

1 Would you like to join us for dinner?

Are you allergic to anything?

Can we take you out for lunch?

Can you stay for lunch today?

Do you need any help with the menu?

Could you recommend something else?

Is there anything I need to know before I make a reservation?

2
1	love	3	like	5	sounds / is
2	would	4	afraid		

3

1 I've never tasted anything quite like this before.

2 Compliments to the chef!

3 The meal was fabulous!

4 Thank you for bringing me here.

5 It's been a wonderful experience.

6 I couldn't possibly eat another thing.

4
1	ingredients	3	course	5	dessert
2	vegetarian	4	fruity	6	spicy

5 1 **Meg:**   Anja, would you like to join us for dinner?

2 **Anja:**   I'd like that very much.

3 **Meg:**   There's a restaurant just around the corner from your hotel that serves fantastic local dishes. Do you like lamb?

4 **Anja:**   Actually, I'm a vegetarian. I hope that won't be a problem.

5 **Meg:**   Not at all. We can go to another restaurant. Is there anything else I need to know before I make a reservation?

6 **Anja:**   No, I eat everything else. What time shall we say?

7 **Meg:**   How about 7:30? I'll wait for you in the hotel lobby.

8 **Anja:**   Perfect.

6 **Model answers**

1 Yes, that would be nice.

2 Well, I don't eat meat. I'm a vegetarian. / No, I eat everything.

3 Perfect. I'll see you then.

11 Tell us a story

1 1 remember   2 tell   3 say   4 forget

2 1 S   3 B   5 C   7 E
       2 E   4 B   6 C   8 S

3 1 nightmare   5 believe   9 hurt
       2 surprised   6 joking   10 happened
       3 terrifying   7 right
       4 serious   8 Lucky

4

1 What a nightmare! / You can't be serious! / I don't believe it! / You must be joking! / You're kidding, right? / So what happened?

2 What a nightmare! / You can't be serious! / I don't believe it! / You must be joking! / You're kidding, right? / So what happened?

3 What a nightmare! / Sounds terrifying. / You can't be serious! / I don't believe it! / You must be joking! / You're kidding, right? Were you hurt? / So what happened?

4 What a nightmare! / You can't be serious! / I don't believe it! / You must be joking! / You're kidding, right? / So what happened?

12 Sensitive topics

1

1 wrong   **2** rude   **3** insensitive   **4** inconsiderate

2

1 To tell you the truth, I wouldn't know.
2 To be honest, I'd prefer not to talk about it.
3 You know, I really couldn't say.
4 This is a little awkward, but we wouldn't normally do that.

3

1 mind   **3** Forget   **5** matter
2 worry   **4** need   **6** common

4

1 had   **4** mean
2 feels/gets; give/send   **5** understand
3 think; apologize

5 **Model answers**

1 Actually, I'd prefer not to talk about it.
2 This is a little embarrassing, but we don't normally do that.
3 I apologize. You must think I'm terribly insensitive.

13 Goodbye – for now!

1
1 Give
2 see
3 Feel
4 look
5 hope
6 be

2
1 So
2 Right then
3 that (the) time
4 Well
5 Anyway

3
1 Would you excuse me for a moment?
2 If you'll excuse me, I have to make a phone call.
3 Excuse me for a moment. I have to take care of something.

4
1 rush
2 going
3 be
4 seeing
5 coming
6 been

5
1 b
2 c
3 f
4 e
5 a
6 d
7 h
8 g

6 **Model answers**
1 I'd better be going if I want to catch my flight.
2 If you'll excuse me, I have to make a phone call.
3 Is that the time? I'm afraid I really should get going.
4 I have to rush. It's been great to talk to you again.
5 Thanks for coming. I hope to see you at next year's conference.

14 Phone, video and online meetings

1

1 Can we all say our names so we know who's here?

2 Let's get started. Does everyone have the agenda?

3 That's it for today. Thank you everyone.

4 You should really try to make the next meeting in person.

5 OK, can everyone hear?

6 We've all just had lunch together.

2 **a** 5   **b** 1   **c** 6   **d** 2   **e** 4   **f** 3

3 **1** d   **2** c   **3** a   **4** b

4 **1** behind   **3** ahead   **5** right
     2 difference   **4** morning

5 **1** let; get   **3** running   **5** caught
     2 want; keep   **4** talking   **6** leave

6 **Model answers**

1 Actually, you've caught me at a bad time. I was just about to leave.

2 We're four hours ahead. It's 18:00 here.

3 Thanks, Nathan. I'll let you get back to work!

15 Email exchanges

1 Model answers

1 Hope you're not too busy.
2 I hope you're enjoying the weather.
3 How are you doing?
4 How's work?

2 Model answers

1 Looking forward to seeing you again.
2 Have a great weekend.
3 Bye for now.
4 All the best
5 Take care.
6 Thanks again for your hospitality.

3 Model answers

It was great to meet you.
It was great to meet the team.
It was great to see you again.
It was great to talk to you.
It was great to visit your offices.
It was great to learn more about your business.

4

1 ✓   2 ✓   7 ✓

5 Model answers

1 Thank you very much for your hospitality. It was really great to meet you in person at last. And I really liked your open-plan offices – the location is amazing and so is the city.
2 Thanks again for everything.
3 All the best
   Lisa

16 Social media for professionals

1
1 remember   3 remember   5 remember
2 remind   4 remember

2
1 invitation   3 connect
2 touch   4 close; instead

3
1 a   3 e   5 h   7 f
2 g   4 d   6 b   8 c

4
1 I thought this might interest you.
2 Have you seen this article?
3 I thought of you when I read this.
4 Is this of any use to you?

5
1 sharing   2 reading   3 know

6 **Model answer**

Hi Barbara

You may not remember me, but we spoke briefly at the conference in Toronto last week.

I saw you were on LinkedIn® and thought it would be good to get in touch. Would you like to connect?

Kind regards

Claude

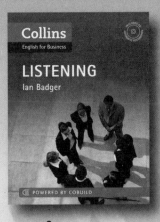
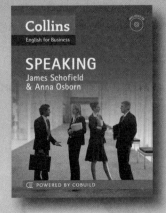
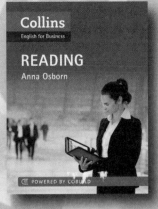
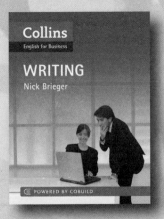